THE SHOEMAKER: Principles & Guide for Professionals

Dandy Ahuruonye

Published by Dandy Ahuruonye, 2023.

THE SHOEMAKER: PRINCIPLES & GUIDE FOR PROFESSIONALS

First edition. August 22, 2023.

ISBN: 979-8223438793

Written by Dandy Ahuruonye.

Also by Dandy Ahuruonye

THE WHISPERING POET: An Anthology of Igbo And Other Proverbs
Grocc-ofly
Reading Glasses for Mama Eagle
The Cute Kids of Madugascar
Nora never gave up
A Fishhook and the Riverboy
Positive Brainwash
Groccolli
The Adventures of Groccolli
Happyville
Oh, What a Mars!
Stinky and The Dung Beetle
The Gull Who Must be Obeyed
THE SHOEMAKER: Principles & Guide for Professionals

Watch for more at https://wordpress.com/home/
dandyahuruonye.wordpress.com.

THE SHOEMAKER:
Principles & Guide
For Professionals

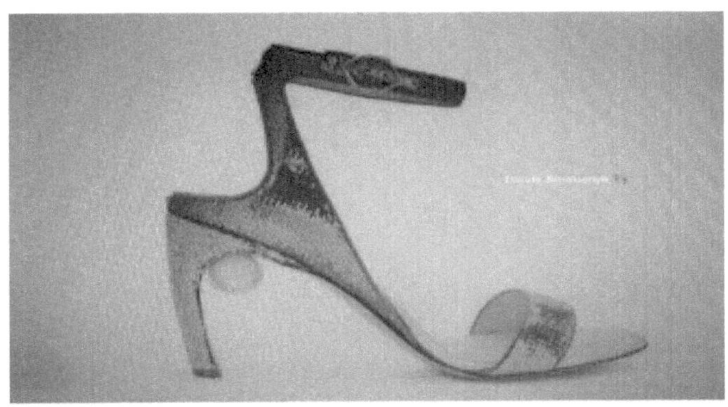

DANDY
AHAOMA AHURUONYE

ISBN:

   DANDY AHURUONYE

COPYRIGHT

ABOUT THE AUTHOR

THE SHOEMAKER: Principles & Guide for Professionals is a technical guidebook, written and produced by Dandy Ahuruonye. It is his latest addition to the growing list of publications that are now available at Dandy Ahuruonye Books.

Dandy designed this manuscript to serve as a simplified manual for anyone desiring to become a professional shoe designer - without the need to initially serve as an apprentice at a master's workshop. Armed with this handbook, you can become a shoe designer, even though you never went to any of today's designing schools.

After completing his studies in Fashion Designing, Ahuruonye set up a designing studio. From there, he built high-end custom-made footwear. At the peak of his creative prowess, he successfully designed a kit for a First Lady. That was during his renowned 'Designer's Finger' period.

DEDICATED:

To my long-suffering instructor – the late **Christian Amaram**. *Dede*, you were a great mentor, a gentle coach, and a loving guardian.

To my cousin and former business partner, **Ezekiel Okeogu**. *Ezie*, my alliance with you gave me the crucial first wings, which helped me to navigate the perilous risks that most budding artists encounter.

To you **Misheal Adolphus Erondụ**, for generously providing me with full boarding during the precarious period when I was an impecunious student at the designing school.

Mr **David Amalaha** (my first member of staff & manager), and

Mr **Udochi Enweremmadụ** (2nd Designer's Finger Graduate

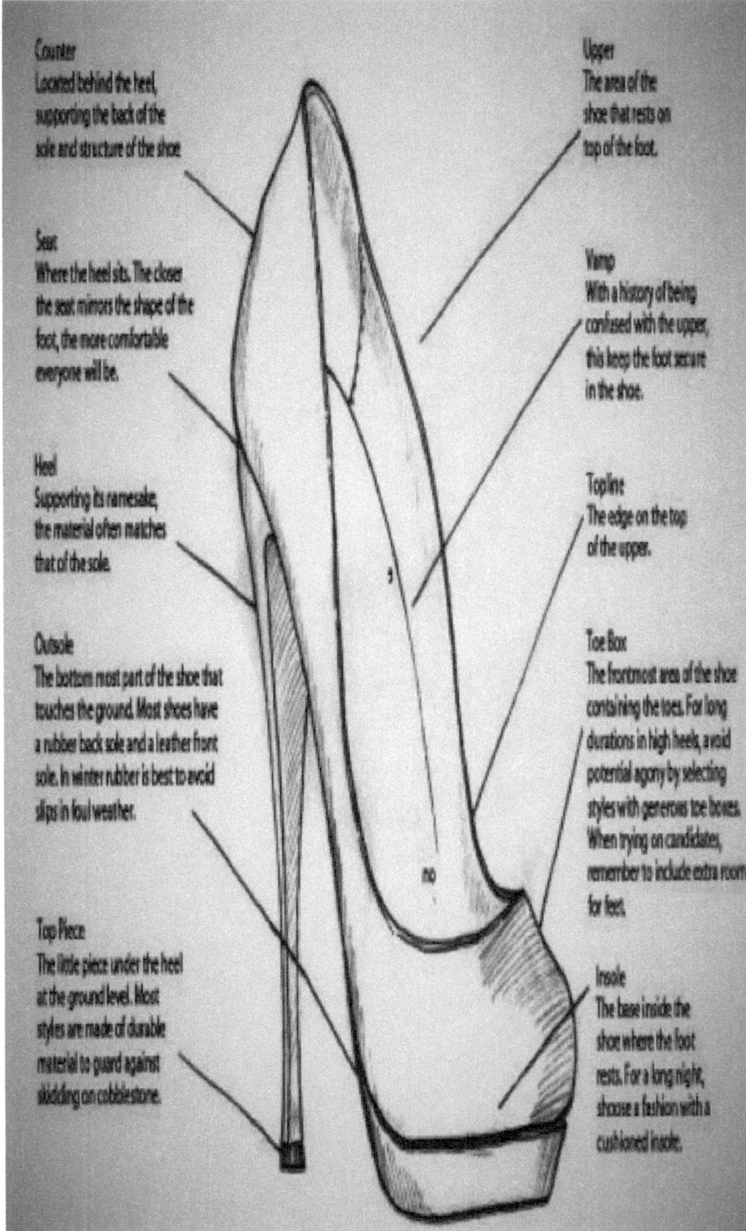

OVERVIEW

My determination to preserve the esteemed, but age-old craft of making shoes using bare hands, inspired the writing of this manual.

What I regard as the **manufacturing rebellion** - but which other people call the industrial revolution – has become a substitute to the old village shoemaker.

Today, I observe, with a measure of chagrin, the large, mechanised factories filled with armies of workers. But regrettably, each human-machine in these industrial units knows only one mode of operation involved in the process that leads to producing footwear. It is therefore painful for me to contemplate that some of these shoe factory workers may view themselves as **shoemakers** – but nothing could be further from the truth!

REFERENCES

L ondon College Of Fashion
    University Of The Arts London
National Library of Ireland, Dublin
Tomas Bata University, Zlín, CR
Tallaght Library, Tallaght, Ireland
Bata Shoes Industry, Aba, Nigeria
William Jay Bowerman, Nike, Inc.
Shoe Gurus Sir White & Paucity
Footwear Design & Development,
Lasell University, Massachusetts
Edited By: dandyahuruonyebooks.com
Artwork/Interior: dandyahuruonyebooks.com
Dandy Ahuruonye planned all design concepts and methods presented herein.

Dandy Ahuruonye

1: ABOUT THIS MANUAL

I designed this manual to guide you from being a rooky, or absolute novice, to a professional shoemaker within a short time. The aim is to help you become a professional without ever having to serve as an apprentice to a master. From the first chapter, this guidebook first provides basic information and guides from a beginner's point of view. As I went through the difficulty of learning how to make shoes from just an oral and practice tutorial; I realised that there is a crucial need for a published guide to supplement the hands-on apprentice training in the workshop.

This profession of making footwear by hand is one that only needs three things: **practice**, **practice**, and more **practice**. At the outset, plan to make a few pairs of shoes, so that you can improve through regular practice.

If you are very positive and use this manuscript regularly, chances are your first pair would be fairly wearable; even so, you will need to improve on your initial achievements. After making thousands of shoes by exclusively using my bare hands, it became clear to me that the D.I.Y approach to shoemaking is possible; actually, it is the way forward.

Therefore, this guidebook aims to encourage more people to make and wear custom footwear. Doing this day after day for more than a dozen years inspired me to prepare simple rudimentary steps to design and build footwear - from the very first steps to more advanced and authentic methods. Still, my overall goal remains the same: To help many people create practical and comfortable shoes either for commercial or for personal use – Doing so *one pair at a time*.

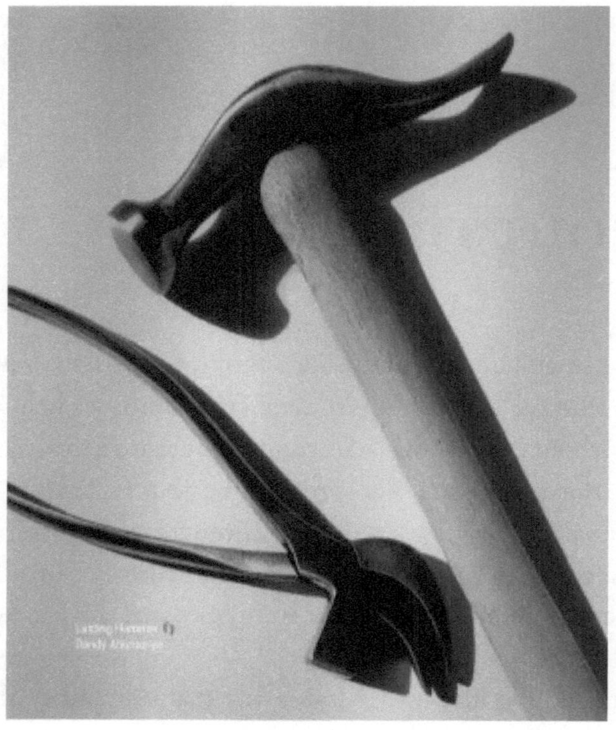

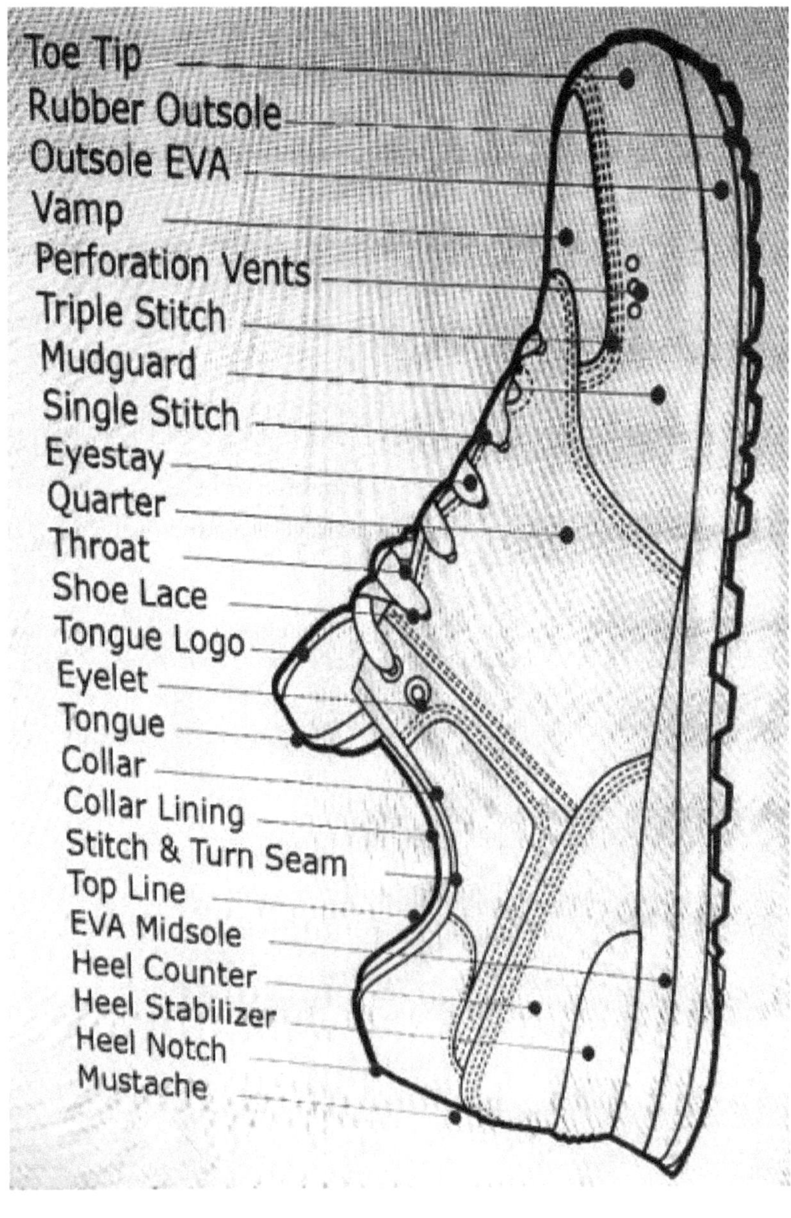

I AM CONVINCED THAT this manual will help you – not just to avoid some of the same troubles most beginners encounter, but also to train you to become the professional shoe designer that you didn't know you could become.

There are many reasons handmade shoes are very problematic to make and, by implication, very expensive to purchase. One reason is that the designer has to be trained extensively before he or she can become a Tailor, Tanner, Machinist, Smoother, Knitter, Laster, and Coupler all at once; to be able to competently produce a pair of shoes using bare hand. Consequently, handmade shoes require specialised skills if they are to have very good quality, look presentable, and at the same time, be truly comfortable for the wearer.

I would like to demonstrate how to produce a pair of fine, high-quality shoes by hand with minimal – if any – use of machinery.

To make our pair, the designer must be well practised and trained. This enables him or her to be able to either carry out all the actions required to produce a pair of fine shoes as outlined in this manual or be in a position where he can direct someone else on what to do to achieve the same result.

NB: ALL INSTRUCTIONS in this manual are for a right-handed person!

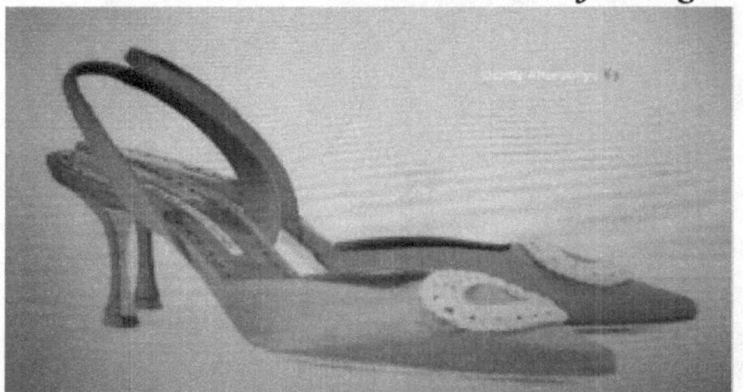

2: SECTIONS OF SHOE CONSTRUCTION

Step 1: Leather
    Leather Material Leather Selection
Identifying Pattern Pieces
Step 2: Cutting
Quarter Vamp Lining
Heel Lining Binding
Heel Counter Insole
Step 3: Sub-Assembly
Skiving Heel Counter
Moulding Heel Counter
Skiving Leather Pieces
Prepare Lining for Stitching
Step 4: Stitching
Stitching Lining & Binding Prepare for Folding
Top Stitch Binding to Quarter Attach Quarter to Vamp
Stitch Quarter to Vamp
Step 5: Findings
Hardware: Rivets, Eyelets Speed-Lacing
Final Step Sub-Assembly
Remove Moulded Heel Counter
Step 6: Lasting Cement Construction
Heel Counter Mould Toe Cap
Final Steps
Cement Construction
Hand Lasting Completed

Pulling Upper
Step 7: Bottom Work
Cementing Cork Filler
Developing Outsole Units
Attach Midsole to Shoe
Remove Shoe from Shoe Last
Attach Outsole
Step 8: Finishing
Sanding
Apply Finish to Leather
Insert Foot Bed & Lacing
Finished Shoe

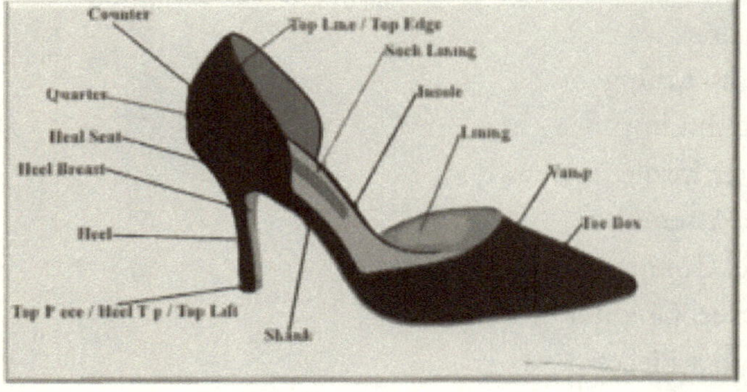

3: NAMES OF SHOE PARTS

Before you even take your very first step, I would like you to pause and inspect some of the key parts that make up a shoe. The following list shows the names of most parts of contemporary footwear; this list is not presented in any particular order. Knowing these names will benefit those who are perhaps looking to move up to the higher echelon of shoemaking; still, it is handy to be able to refer to this if and when needed.

Arch - The area of the insole of a shoe that is padded, with the sole aim of supporting the arch of the foot.

Back Seam - A perpendicular layer for attaching the quarters for support at the middle of the back of a shoe.

Eyelets - Holes in the upper, above the tongue, where shoelaces pass through.

Back Stay - This is a brief trimming of material that connects the quarters down the rear of the shoe.

Collar – A padded strip of material attached to the opening or topline of the shoe.

Foxing – This refers to a piece of trimming (usually leather) fitted on top of, or into the rear quarters.

Counter – This is a reinforced piece of cardboard, leather, plastic, or other strong but flexible material that is installed between the shoe lining and the upper at the rear of the shoe, immediately above the heel, or rear sole as in the case of a flat shoe.

Facing - The area(s) of the shoe where the eyelets are inserted for the shoelace.

Gore - An elastic panel attached to each side of the vamp to provide a suitable level of comfort for the end-user of the footwear; this can be put on and/or taken off. Depending on the design, the tongue of a shoe shelters the hidden gore and provides extra cosiness.

Heel - The heel of a shoe is an independent piece of material that raises the rearmost part of the shoe.

Mid-sole - A layer of cushioned material between the innersole and outsole, adding additional comfort and support to a shoe.

Inseam - This is a concealed layer of a shoe that connects the insole, welt, lining and Upper

Insole - The layer of material that lies on top of the sole inside a shoe where the bottom of your foot contacts a shoe.

Linings - Various materials usually sheepskin, cloth, or leather that run around the inside of the upper to provide more comfort when the foot is inside the shoe.

Shank - A rigid material (usually metal or plastic) positioned between the insole and the sole of the shoe to supply support.

Sole - The part of the shoe that sits below the wearer's foot. The upper and sole make up the entire shoe.

Outsole - The part of the sole that touches the ground, usually made of leather or rubber.

Plug - The sewn-in vamp on a loafer. Usually defined as a plug if the material or texture differs from the rest of the shoe.

Puff - Reinforcement inside the upper at the toe of a shoe to give it shape and support.

Quarter - The back half of the upper. Attached at the front to the vamp, making up both sides of a shoe, and wrapping around the rear of the shoe. On some shoes, the vamp and the quarter are a single piece of leather.

Upper - The part of a shoe that covers the entire topside of a shoe; and depending on the shoe design, the upper may also cover the sides and rear of the foot.

Throat - The area of the shoe where the top cap ends, or the area where the base of the tongue is attached to the vamp.

Toe cap - A 1-to-2-millimetre-thick piece of leather that sits between the shoe upper and the leather lining. Provides the toe of the shoe with an elegant look, preserves the shape, and protects the foot from forces outside of the shoe.

Waist - The section between the in-step and arch.

Tongue - A piece of material, usually leather or cloth, sewn into the vamp of a laced shoe, extending between the throat and the waist of a shoe.

Topline - Also referred to as the Rim or the Collar, it is the top edge of the upper or opening of a shoe.

Vamp - The section of shoe upper covering the forward-facing part of the foot and attaches to the quarter.

Welt - The piece of material for joining the upper to the sole.

AS YOU READ THROUGH this guidebook, you are going to see that a more detailed description of most of these parts is presented; along with their role and application. Therefore, when you encounter the same names or descriptions elsewhere in this book, do not view it as repetition; this list is just a quick way to help you memorise the names and short definitions of these shoe parts.

Assorted Tools ©
Dandy Ahuruonye

4: BASIC SHOEMAKING TOOLS

LAST, LEATHER, LINING Material (Usually Very Soft Leather) Sole, Heel
Fibre Material, Shanks, Insoles
A Hammer, A Pair of Pliers, A Pair of Pincers, And A Chisel
A Single-Edge Channel Knife with Razor Blades
Tack Nails or Brass, And Clinching Nails
Welt (Depending on Chosen Design)
Strong Glue (Or Barge Cement)
Gum or Other Adhesives, Duct Tape, A Rasp
A Small Stove or A High Wattage Electric Bulb (As a Source of Heat)
A Stainless-Steel Spoon for Leather Dressings (Heated Using the Stove)
Nylon Thread for Sewing
A Large Sewing Needle, Candles and Wax (To Make Thread Easy to Use).

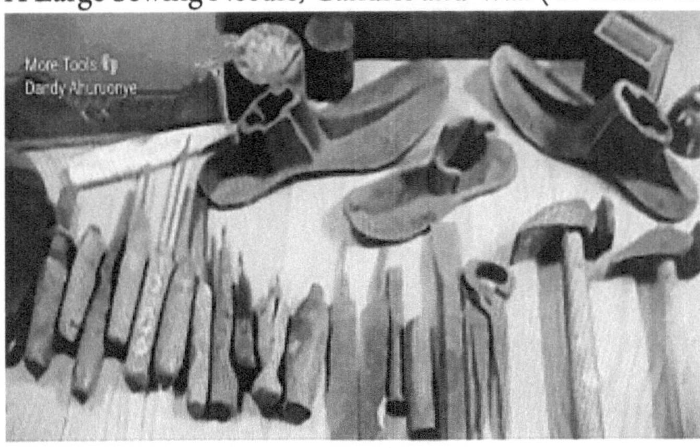

DESCRIPTION OF BASIC TOOLS

Knives - Shorter ones are good for channel cutting and clicking; while we use the longer ones for shaping soles, insoles, heels, etc.

Lasting Pincers – Also known as Footwear Lasting Pliers, with built-in hammer face. For shoe lasting and sole nailing. Often, the hammer face is made of plastic or wood.

French Hammer - No nail leaves marks on it, it is good for all sorts of jobs, like putting in or removing lasting nails, pegs, pegging awl, heel nails, inner nails, brass nails, etc.

Nail pliers - Good for cutting long nails, remove them - even from inside the shoe (sometimes it is a very handy item in courses).

Talcum powder - Gently apply powder on the Last before Lasting, it can be very handy when you want to prevent the Last from being stuck in the shoe; this happened to me a few times in my early days. It can also be useful for sewing, as it prevents nylon thread friction.

Lasting nails.

A leather container for the small things, like awls, bone folder, sharpening stone, and stuff like those.

You also need - Rubber cement, Sole glue, Wheat past

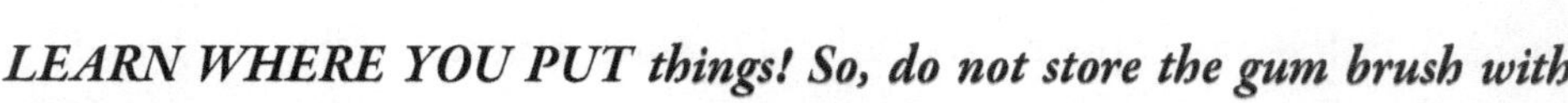

LEARN WHERE YOU PUT things! So, do not store the gum brush with other tools or materials; it always ends in tears.

5: SHOE CONSTRUCTION

Shoe construction has hardly changed in the last three to four hundred years. The best masters build the finest handmade shoes using various high-quality materials. In most cases, it takes about twenty to thirty-five individual parts to produce a pair of fine ladies' shoes. In that case, the customer receives a high-quality overall product, one that guarantees her years of satisfaction and comfort.

When people refer to making a shoe as 'shoe construction,' they are referring to a hugely painstaking and complicated procedure. From the tip of the heel (top lift) to the front stiff (toe cap); each piece and section of customised footwear is assembled in sequence - one after the other.

A shoe is made up of two main sections or parts. The first is the shaft or the upper, and the other is the base or bottom (Ground Force).

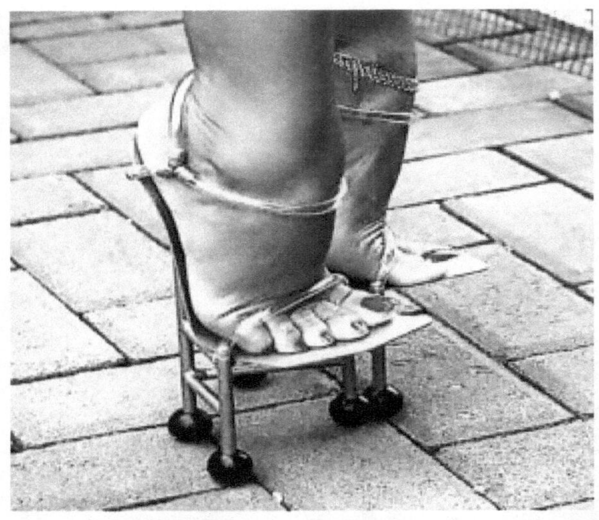

6: INTRODUCTION

A shoe is an item of footwear designed with the primary aim of safeguarding and providing some level of comfort for the foot of a human being. From a comfort point of view, then, we produce footwear for fashion and decoration. Furthermore, shoes are now being designed for other specific needs such as skiing, cycling, playing football, climbing, and running.

In special cases, we can build footwear for people with orthopaedic needs, or for those who have an arthritic impairment. Culture, fashion evolution and warmth, outdoor and military needs, and sheer individual taste - have all combined to enormously influence what people wear on their feet today. However, shoes were originally designed to focus especially on functionality.

Shoes are to the feet what a garment is to the body, but your footwear does much more than that. They provide comfort while on the move; and safeguard the foot against menaces on the ground below.

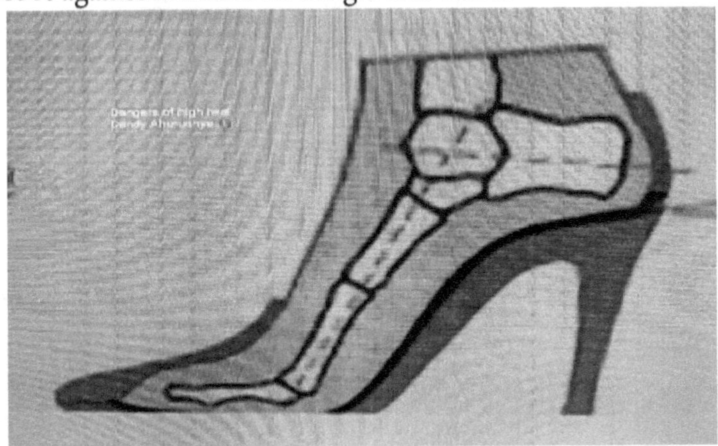

Interestingly, the days are long gone when shoes were viewed simply as bodyguards for the feet. Today, a pair of custom-made footwear has become more of a fashion statement. As an expert custom shoemaker, one of the first parts of the body that I glance at whenever I meet a person is his or her feet.

At one corporate Annual General Meeting a few years ago, I observed with fondness as a youthful and animated CEO addressed the large gathering while showing off an unmistakable pair of handmade pointed shoes. Not surprisingly, his entire fitted attire - which also included a blue Hugo Boss costume - spoke volumes about the type of station he occupied in life.

Therefore, your choice of footwear tells observers about your culture, ethos, position, the type of environment you operate in, and at times, what nationality you represent.

Shoe designs have grown into wide-ranging forms because of the influence of father time, master art, doctor music, teacher literature, and mother culture.

For many, an exceptional emphasis is on appearance more than anything else. However, the emergence of the powerful fashion industry in recent decades has single-handedly dictated many design elements we see in modern footwear.

Contemporary footwear shows a clear discrepancy when compared to its older cousins - in terms of cost, style, complexity, and range. Uncomplicated flip-flops may comprise just a reedy sole, simple straps and buckles; and are sold for just a few euros. On the other hand, high-end fashion shoes built by prominent master designers, using high-end expensive materials, may involve intricate and painstaking construction. These can be sold from a few hundred, up to several thousand euros per pair.

MOST OFTEN, THESE TYPES of shoes are designed and built with a particular purpose in mind; when that is the case, we refer to the end product as **custom-made footwear**

7: BESPOKE OR CUSTOM-MADE

Each time you look to buy premium shoes or want a shoe expert to build a pair for you by using a procedure beyond the usual basic robotic construction, you will come across various jargons that are used to underline the level of craftsmanship that is involved in such an undertaking. Many specialist shoe craftsmen and women use terms that aren't known by those outside this industry; one of those terms is 'benchgrade,' which means the primary step up from uncomplicated automated shoe construction. As this word suggests, the term is a combination of two terms - bench and grade and gives the idea that producing shoes without involving an automated process starts on a seat and bench. That is why such a hands-on approach to shoemaking is laborious; but in the end, it results in what we may refer to at times as bespoke shoes. Therefore, it is extremely important that – should one decide to produce a pair of handmade footwear, then no expense should be spared. Think about it! It wouldn't make any sense at all to go through the challenge of Lasting shoes by hand, Welting shoes by hand, and building insoles by hand and not use exotic skins and top-grade leather to complete such a personalised construction.

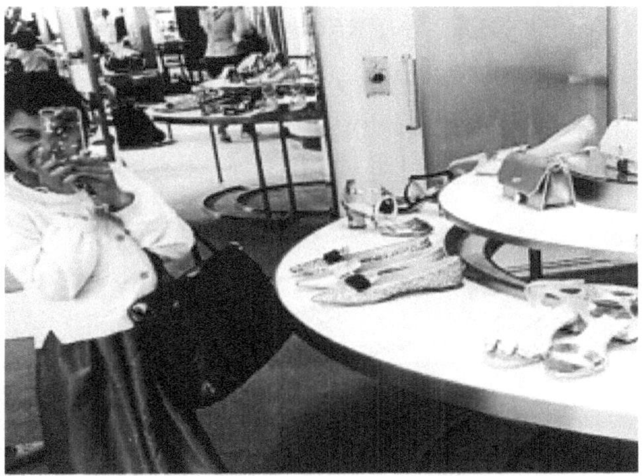

TOP CONTEMPORARY DESIGNERS:

Among the list of top contemporary designers that produce some of the best and most expensive footwear by hand; one pair at a time, are:

Andrew McDonald

Andrew formerly worked at **John Lobb** in London, and also at **Hermès** in Paris. Andrew builds shoes for both men and women that have a distinctly Aussie feeling, with an uncompromising dedication to quality.

Berluti makes shoes piece by piece, and each piece of material is cut by

hand, stitched by hand, and even polished by hand.   As much of a status symbol as they are striking, his bespoke shoes are very expensive. Therefore, if you desire a pair of shoes from Berluti footwear, you'll have to pay dearly. Still, it would be worth it for the heads you are going to turn when you wear their pair.

CAROLINE GROVES

Caroline is dedicated to giving women the excellence, durability, and high fashion they demand. Her shoes are strictly for those who are concerned or obsessed with only one thing in life - **SHOES!**

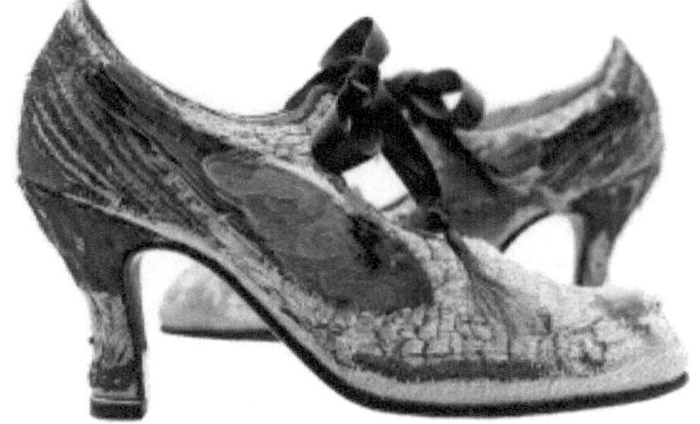

Ludwig Reiter, Vienna

Ludwig has been making Goodyear-welted shoes in true Viennese flair for some time now.

George Cleverley

George himself had a hand in the making of almost every pair. He is a highly respected name that has some of the most exacting standards in the specialist footwear industry. To buy a pair of footwear stamped with the George Cleverley logo, you may have to pay a king's ransom; but you will be walking on air from the very moment you put on a pair of his shoes!

JIMMY CHOO

Designer Jimmy became famous due to his unique style, as well as the quality of his footwear creations; all handmade shoes for women.

Choo's background gave him an upper hand over his competitors as the fashion designer relied on the craftsmanship, he learned from his father, who was a cobbler, to build some of the most outrageous and coveted female shoes in the world. This means that he was immersed in the world of shoemaking from an early age, and it shows in the styles he meticulously and subtly injects into each pair he makes. Little wonder that his long list of clients included Renee Zellweger, Princess Diana, and Julia

Roberts, just to mention a few.

DOWN THROUGH THE AGES, shoes have generally been made using leather or wooden materials. This has changed in recent decades with the emergence of such cheap and easy-to-acquire materials as rubber, plastics, and other materials derived from petrochemical sources.

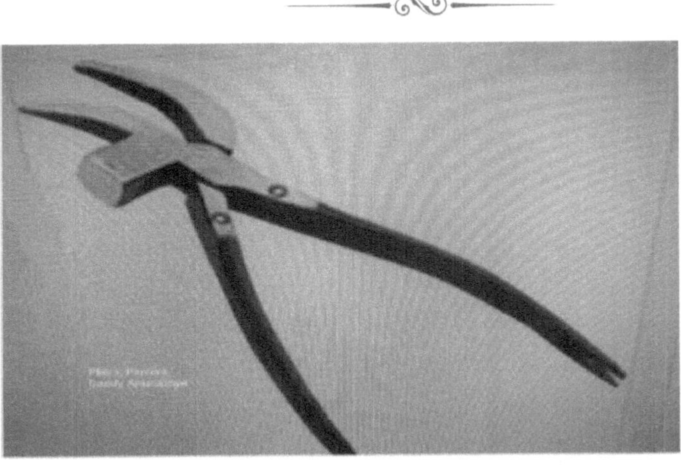

PLASTIC HAS PLAYED the biggest role in driving down the cost of shoes, while at the same time also raising its quality and durability. Rubber has also made it easier to construct shoes of various kinds - from the simple - to the psychedelic. Therefore, the custom shoemakers who in this hi-tech age still seek to construct footwear by hand using leather, a hammer, adhesive, and nails are to be admired.

THE ART OF BESPOKE shoemaking is slowly becoming extinct, especially in Europe and North America. Nevertheless, there is still a large army of artisan shoemakers who are steadfastly keeping this very important craft and tradition alive, especially in **Aba**, Eastern Nigeria. This industry - powered exclusively by bare hands and some willpower, is very important - not just because of being a source of livelihood for thousands of families; but also for aesthetic reasons.

A local Shoemaker in Ariaria, Aba

FOR EXAMPLE - HAVE you ever dressed up in a pair of personalised shoes customised to match the characteristics of each of your feet? If you have, you probably found it hard to wear anything else afterwards. Many who have managed to try out a pair of footwear specially built for their feet would confirm that wearing custom-made shoes contributes valuably towards maintaining healthy feet.

That is why I here present you with a guide on what to expect when creating bespoke footwear.

FOR THE SHOE TO BE truly tailored, you MUST build it specifically to fit each of your client's feet. Made-to-order or personalised means that the shoes should not have a particular known design or size; for example, you cannot say that you are building a size 6 or a size 8 for the client. Instead, you are building a size 'Mary' or a size 'Tom.' Consequently, every custom-made shoe should be labelled as 'size client,' whatever his or her name is. Yes, producing shoes manually is hard work; but it is certainly a labour of love!

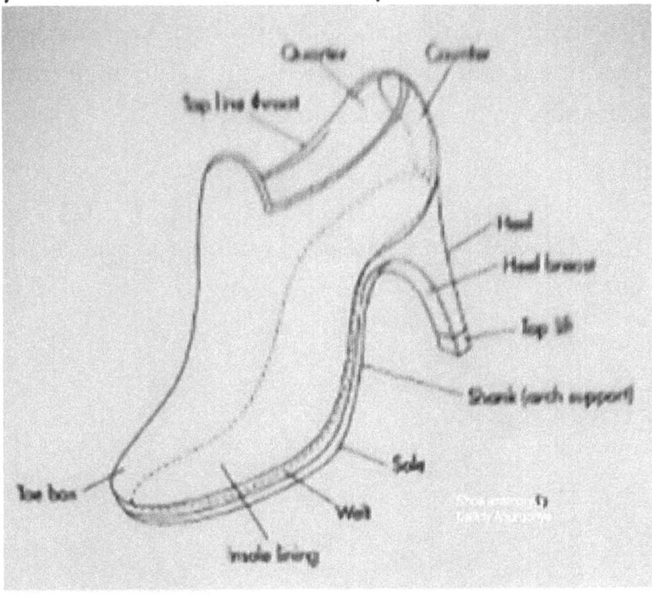

8: SHOEMAKING - STEP BY STEP

Have you ever wondered about the anatomy of the product that protects your feet - commonly known as a pair of shoes? Whether or not you have, let us now review some of the critical parts that make up the pair you are wearing, the pair you are admiring, or the pair you have just bought.

A shoe's anatomy comprises the toe cap, upper, heel, sole, shank, welt, and waist. The most prominent part of shoes is the upper. The upper includes the vamp, tongue, eyelets, throat, puff, quarters and lining.

FOR THE BEST COMFORT of the end-user, you need to capture the actual, live size of each foot!

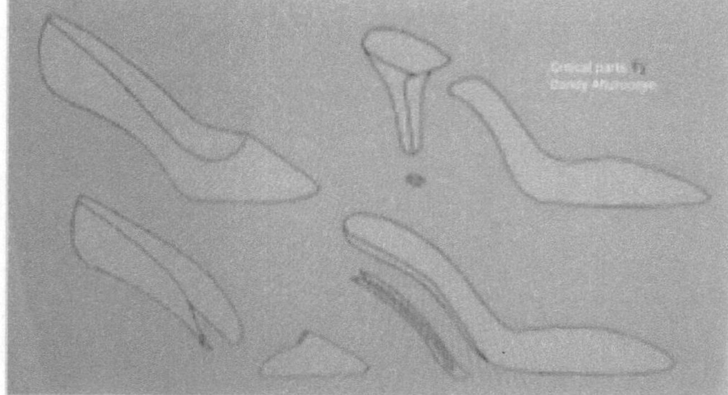

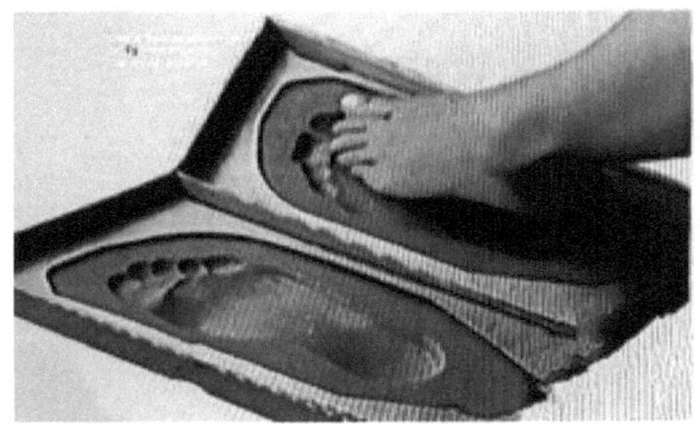

When you become a well-trained, traditional shoemaker, you may decide to build a pair of shoes as a custom-made product. In that case, the best way to start is to arrange to meet the end-user in person so you can mark both of her feet on a piece of paper or other flexible material. This is very important because no two feet are the same, even though they belong to the same individual. So, for this reason, one would first measure the foot individually before cutting out leather materials for the upper part of the shoe according to the size and shape of the foot.

To capture the true size and shape of the foot, you, the specialist, must do the following:

Have the customer remove all socks or stockings, as these can compress the foot or give the wrong measurement.

She must stand in a very relaxed manner, with her full weight (deadweight) evenly spread between both feet.

She should pull her clothing away so that no part of the foot is hidden.

She must not have overgrown toenails sticking out significantly from her toes, as this could negatively affect your effort to capture the actual size of each foot.

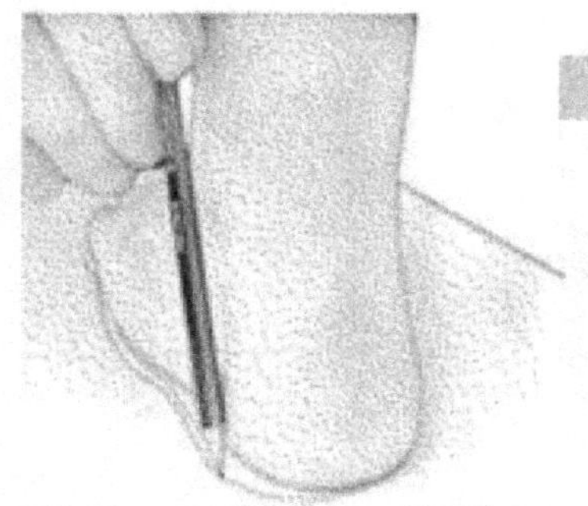
Her full weight must be evenly spread
between both
Dandy

NOW, YOU NEED A SHARPENED pencil. The pencil's tip should be medium to semi-large to allow the mark not to be too small.

When you start drawing, the customer must keep steady with no movement as the foot drawing is a very critical part of making matching and comfortable footwear.

While drawing the foot outline, hold the pencil in a vertical position. Always reach right around the heel as far as is comfortable for your hand to reach and then draw from this position towards yourself and then reach across to access the front of the foot.

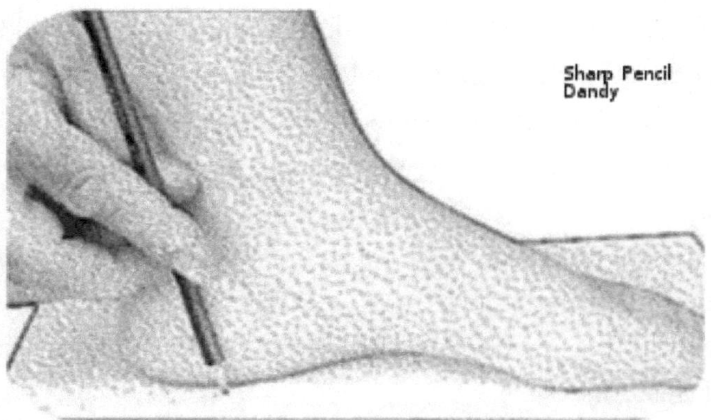
Sharp Pencil
Dandy

Now, go to the starting point and draw back down, again towards yourself, this time from the other side of the foot, to join up with the first line from behind the heel.

NB: IN DESIGNING – especially when making a blueprint or a whiteprint – it is usually easier and more accurate to draw towards your body than away from it.

Reaching around the foot at the start will help you avoid drawing a peak behind the heel which can happen if you start the drawing from behind the heel. This peak, caused by the pencil being held improperly here, will return an inaccurate foot length and diameter measurement.

Accuracy is necessary when using the geometric pattern cutting method, and also for checking the Last against the foot shape.

Once you have her feet marked out correctly, it is time to either make a pair of Lasts to match the shape and size of her feet or visit a professional Last maker with the blueprint of her feet.

This is for him to produce a pair of Lasts that will match her particular size and shape. For a V.I.P client who is able and willing to pay, it is best to take her to a Last maker so that he can use his specialised tools to accurately capture the life-size of each of her feet.

The very next step after this stage would be for you or the client to decide what type of shoes to make.

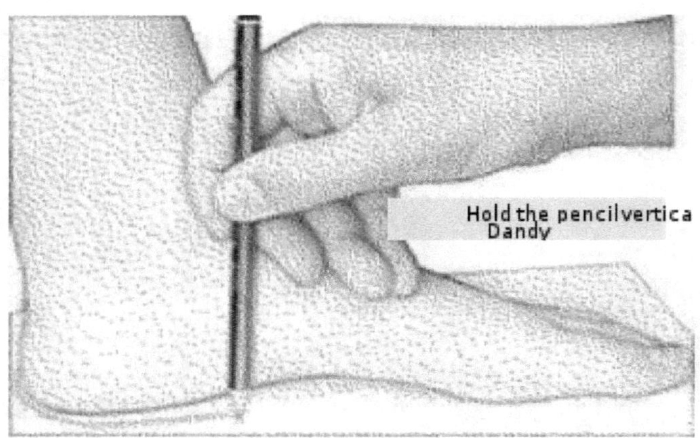
Hold the pencil vertica
Dandy

For example - are you making wholly covered shoes, sandals, boots, high boots, slippers, or other types? She also has to decide on what the core design would be. For example, is she looking for pointed shoes wide front, high heels, flats, soled shoes, open-fronted, moccasin, plain or ornamental design?

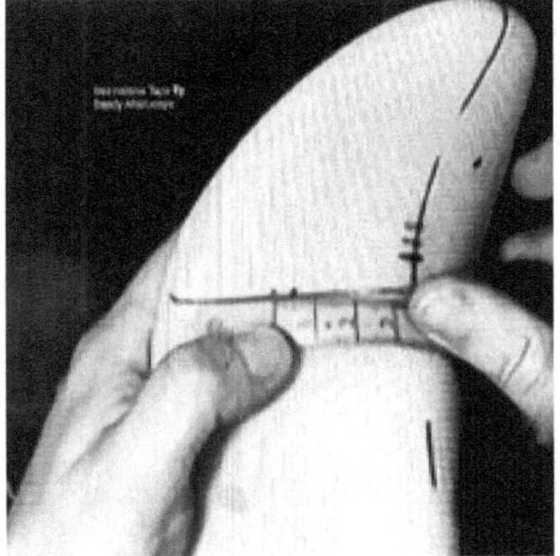

------ ✵ ------

DESIGNS THAT INVOLVE making holes or incisions on the body of the footwear, especially in the case of covered shoes, are notoriously more difficult to make than sandals, or plain shoes that totally cover the foot.

After her choice of design has been agreed upon, quickly sketch it on paper or soft cardboard.

This is very crucial as the quality and appearance of the final product are determined to some extent by what happens during this drawing or blueprint stage involving the upper.

This is when the Shoe Lasts come in handy because at this point, you will need to use them in creating and perfecting key patterns before doing anything else.

Classic shoe Last
Dandy Ahuruonye

9: MEASUREMENTS & TOOLS

As already highlighted, the specialist shoe technician MUST use precise measurements of each foot as an important platform to work from. It means that, even though he is building a 'pair' of shoes, in reality, he is making 'two' individual shoes – one customised for each foot. These are among the key areas that require specific measurement:

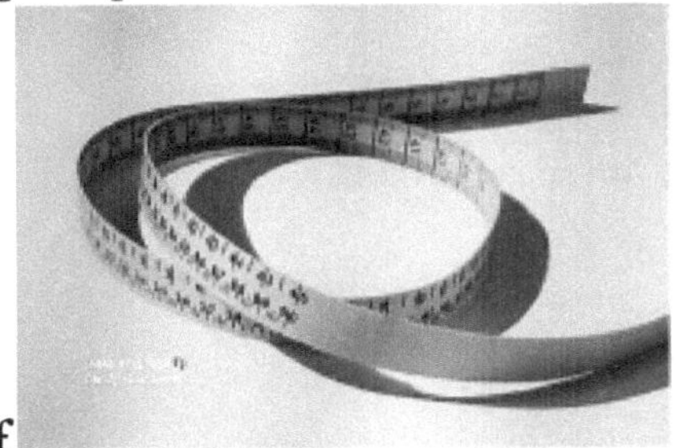

The Calf
The Joint
The Ankle
The Instep
The Under Knee
The Long Heel Line
The Short Heel Line

Some features of the shoes to be made might dictate that certain measurements be taken because of the shoes' specific distinctiveness.

And depending on the design being worked on, a measurement of a particular part of the footwear may be supplemented by the other(s); if and when required.

NOTE: Those who design orthopaedic shoes may at times use a plaster (e.g., Plaster of Paris or P.O.P) cast of the foot in question to refresh their recollections of its characteristics that must be taken into account while the shoe is being completed. But this is unnecessary if you have taken the initial measurements accurately and have secured them in a safe place.

Required Measuring Tools:
A sharp pencil
Firm and flexible paper
Flat board, or memory foam (to stand on)
Dimension stick
A ruler
Narrow tape measure

ALWAYS USE A SKINNY measuring tape because a broad tape measure may not be flexible enough to easily bend with the shape of the foot or the Last. In addition, it helps a lot to use a sharp pencil to mark certain parts of the upper. It would help you to be as accurate as possible.

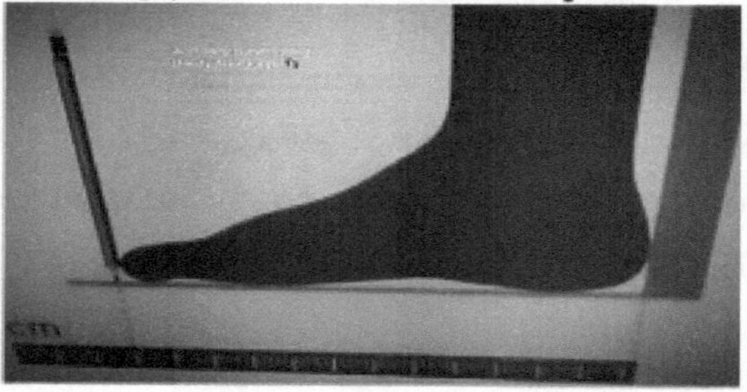

Accuracy saves you time in the long run.

10: THE UPPER or SHAFT

The shaft is intended to cover some or all of the upper part of the foot; this includes parts that are above the sole. A custom shoemaker would normally insist on using very durable but malleable leather - if possible. The upper can be fabricated in some cases (depending on need or specifications) to be combined with some kinds of mesh to allow the feet to breathe. The Form of the upper adds a critical dimension in terms of how the shoes will look and may include zips, laces, buckles, elastic materials, buttons, ornaments, and Velcro.

Parts of The Upper:

VAMP

The vamp starts from the toe cap and extends to the quarter, and/or to the rear of the shoe. Its foremost function is to guard the toes. It should also be designed in such a manner as to catch the attention of both the wearer and

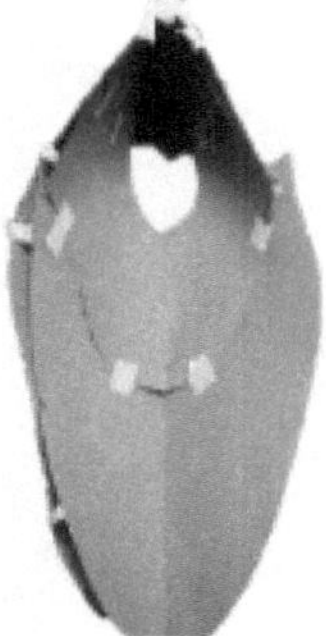

admirers.

Tongue

These are flexible strips of material in shoes that have shoelaces and also contain eyelets.

Eyelets

We provided eyelets for shoes with shoelaces. Those holes allow the shoelace to pass through for tying so that the shoe can firmly grip the foot; Therefore, the tongue is positioned from the vamp towards the throat of the shoe. After the eyelet has been perforated onto the upper of the shoe, you can leave them as they are depending on the quality or texture of the leather material. In most cases though, the eyelets are rimmed using fanciful, but weather-resistant metal or plastic grommets which also allow the holes to maintain their shape and position.

Quarters

The quarters serve as a refuge for the sides and the back of the foot and can go all the way to surround the opening of the shoe. The location of the quarters is immediately behind the vamp. In certain designs, they will proceed around the heel to meet at the shoe lacing point. Depending on the chosen design and finishing, the quarter and the vamp can be made of a single, continuous material; or otherwise separated into different parts. A skilled master may also add foxing, which means another layer that is added to the quarter for supplementary support.

Lining

The lining should be stitched in such a way that you can attach it to the shoe upper from the inside. This layer is permanently present on the inside of the shoe to add support and texture. It MUST be very soft and breathable as this ensures maximum comfort for the user.

The quality of the lining goes a long way in extending the longevity of the shoe.

Throat

The throat determines how much girth can be permitted by the shoe. Therefore, at the front of the vamp, is the throat of the shoe upper, right behind the toe cap, by the main opening of the shoe. It is here, between the central parts of the vamp where the shoe lacing is present, and the quarter, that the different sections are separated by seams. The location of the throat is sometimes referred to as the Eyestay.

Waft

They provide puff-like strengthening to the upper from the inside of the shoe and help maintain the shape of the shoe, particularly around the toe area.

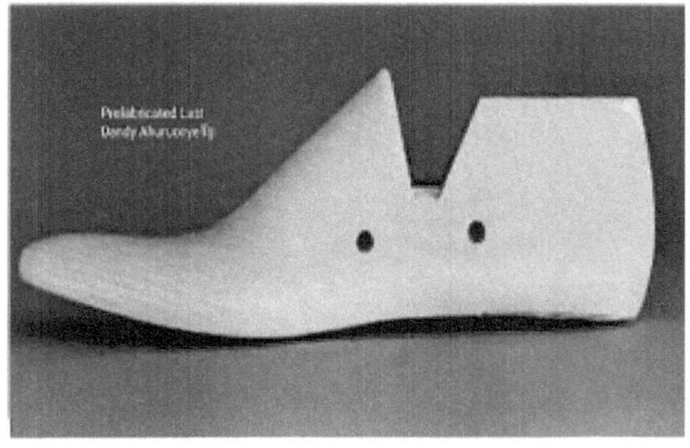
Prefabricated Last
Dandy Aburuoeye'Eji

11: THE MEAN FORME - THE UPPER

By now, you and your client must have selected a Last. Once the Lasts are in place and you are satisfied with them, quickly switch to the next phase. The next consideration that must be settled at this stage is to make the FINAL decision on all the requirements that will determine the exact type of footwear you are going to construct. For example, such decisions as the height of the heel, the toe shape, the specific design, the size and height of the sole, and the type of fit, must all be made NOW.

Armed with a Last and a clear image of the core design of the shoe, we will then begin the creation of the Mean Forme, or otherwise, the fundamental pattern of the upper.

Tools needed in this section include:

The Last & Masking tape

Pencils (one with a small ballpoint, and one with a medium ballpoint)

Tape measure (very narrow)

Knife (a channel knife is a good option)

Flexible ruler (optional)

Dividers (compass)

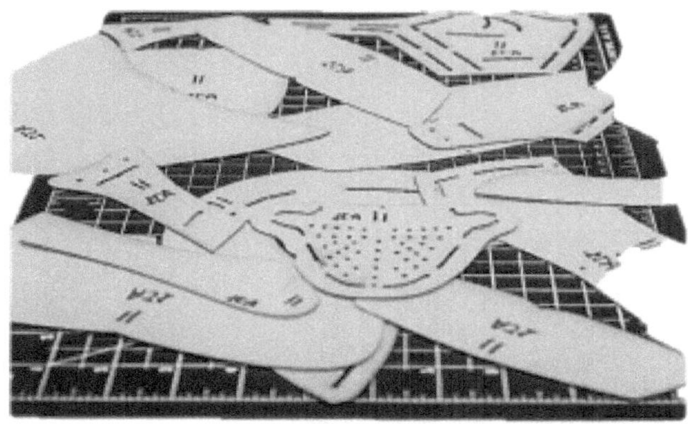

Many custom designers use the shell method to copy the shape and Forme of the Last before constructing the upper part, the sole, and the seat of the shoe.

Using the shell method involves using a stiff plaster of Paris-impregnated cloth. In this technique, a piece of such cloth is cut out and dripped with water until unstiffened.

In this softened state, this piece of cloth is Lasted, using tacks around the bottom and up the back of the Last. When the fabric has dried on the Last, it becomes stiff once more.

Then impress your design on the shell that is on and around the Last and then cut it away. After cutting, the required Forme, or basis for a pattern, is now acquired.

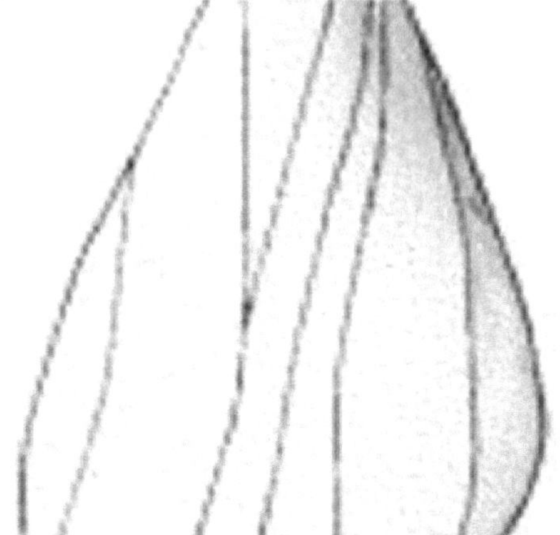

Use masking tape for Forme

However, the most effective method for perfectly copying the shape of the Last, is to use a taped Forme. Adopting this technique is quick and is also known to be flexible. The primary reason for choosing this method is that we can use it with any style of shoe. In all cases, masking tape is the best option; even though there are other methods.

The mean Forme method is a process where the measurement of both the inside and the outside surfaces of the Last are taken. As the Mean Forme of a particular Last is used to create the Standard shape, which is then used to produce the upper patterns for the shoe that is to be made; extreme accuracy (if there is any such thing), must be observed.

Accuracy is the fundamental building block for making patterns; whatever method of pattern acquisition is used.

As some masters would always tell you - *near enough is never good enough!*

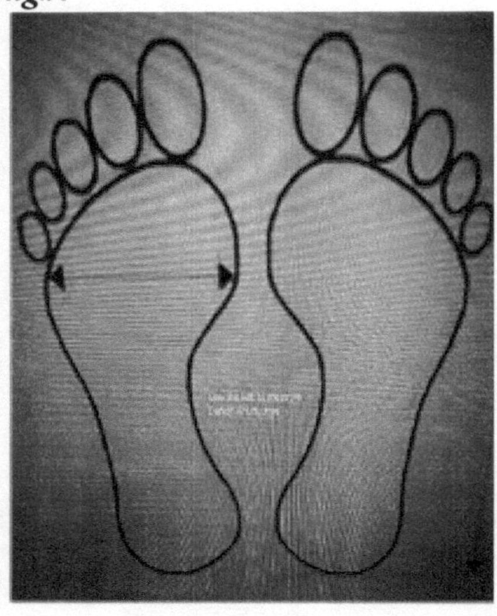

This is because if you are wrong with even half of a millimetre at this stage, that mistake may be compounded at subsequent stages; and if care is not taken, the problem might escalate to where the final upper is too small, or too big and so does not fit the custom Last at all.

Cover the Last with masking tape

THE LAST IS TO BE COVERED. This is done to obtain as close a pattern of the surface of the Last as possible; to enable it to be rendered in two dimensions so that it is possible to create individual pattern pieces out of the Forme.

For some reason, many footwear specialists insist that this process be carried out using the Last moulded out of the customer's left foot.

Use high-quality masking tape to carry out this operation. First, lay a strip down the centre of the front of the Last from the top of its elevated cone to the feather edge at the toe end, and press it into place.

Run another strip down the centre of the back, from top to bottom. All the tape must run over the feather edge to wrap around, and onto the bottom; this will be cut off later.

The Last is to be fully covered with tape

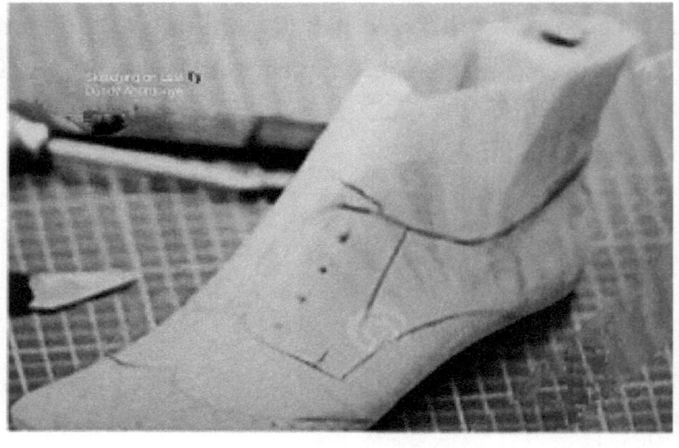

THE STRIPS ARE LAID on from the front to the back first so that when the covering is peeled away at the end; it comes off as a single piece. Each strip must overlap the previous one by about half. Keep doing this until the inside of the Last is covered completely.

If the strips leave gaps because of the shape of the Last, then just tear off more strips to cover them; but make sure that the existing pieces and the centre strips are overlapping each other.

Now cover the outside of the Last in the same manner, overlapping the centre tape at the front, and crossing the strip at the back. The next action is to cover the Last with the tape running across it, from the right angles to the centred tape. Start at the toe and work towards the rear.

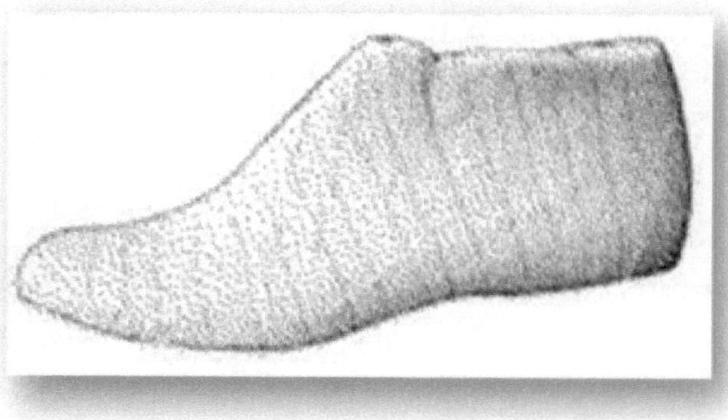

Fully covered Last

These strips overlap by half, as did the others. If the shape of the Last alters your effort to place the tape in straight lines, then use shorter pieces to fill any gaps; but the whole masking tape cover must be complete with two layers. The aim is to reduce the possibility of the mask stretching and becoming distorted.

If the crosswise strips of tape are laid across the Last before the longitudinal strips, then peeling off the masking tape becomes very difficult; even though you can still be able to do this - but with more effort and utmost care.

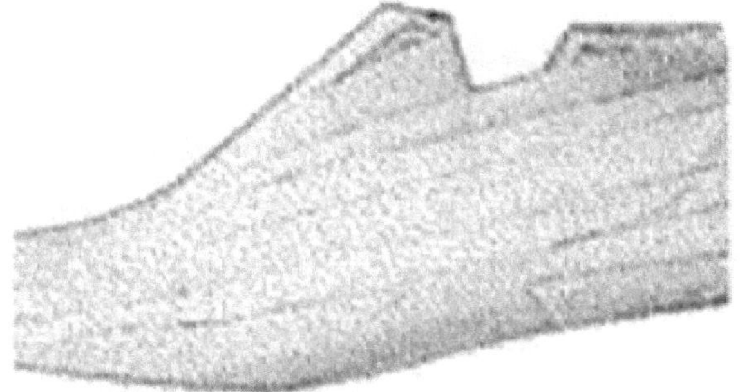

Note: If two layers are not applied, then the tape may stretch once removed, and may yield an inaccurate pattern.

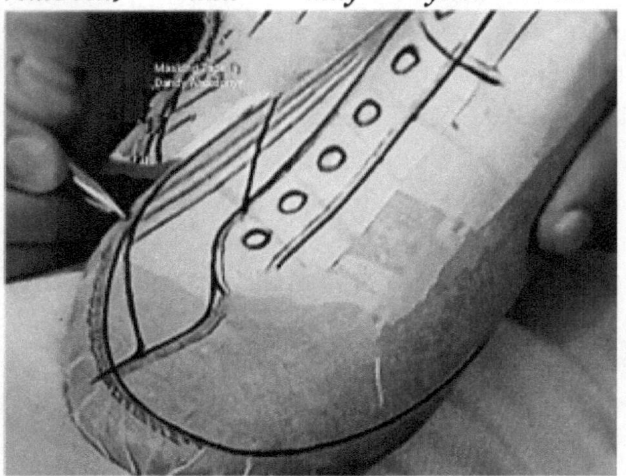

Creating A Pattern Using The Forme

To create a pattern using the blueprint of one of the Lasts moulded out of her feet, first make another copy of the Forme and store that in a safe place just in case you make a mistake with one copy then you have a second to fall back on. With the blueprint, mark out another pattern on very soft but strong material.

Cut out this drawing; and before doing this, manually add about one inch all around it, making it look much larger than the initial marking. Split the drawing in the middle just over halfway towards the front. You can also make other small incisions on the edges, or on other parts of the Forme as you may deem necessary; this is to allow the material to hug the Last perfectly.

Note: Be sure not to split the material into two parts!

The incision(s) will allow you to be able to stick the blueprint around the Last to create the actual pattern for the shoes you are making.

WITH VERY STEADY HANDS, use your marker to draw an impression of the chosen design on the Forme.

Note: You must use a marker with a different colour to that used initially to mark the customer's feet on the material, or else there might be confusion.

When you are satisfied that you have made the correct markings on the Forme material, remove it from the Last and cut away any excesses from the blueprint. There is no harm in sticking the blueprint once more on the Last just to be sure you are on the right track.

Mistakes made at this point would be very difficult to correct later on.

If after sticking the blueprint on the Last a second time you feel the design, and/or the marking(s) requires some adjustment, now is the best time to do that.

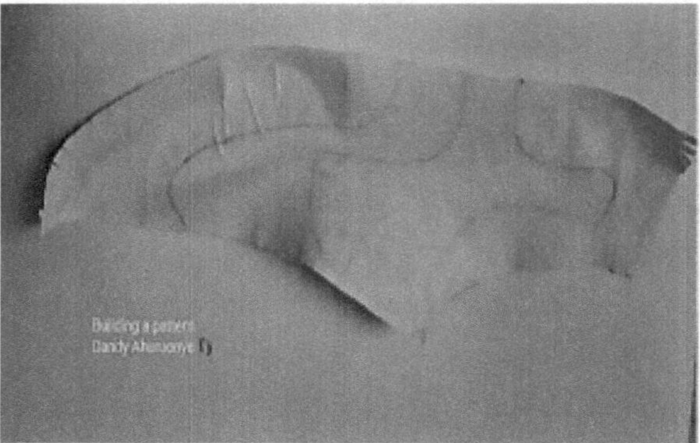

Once you are sure that the blueprint is what you are looking for, remove it and cut away any surplus material on the edges; then make a copy of this blueprint on a larger material.

Do not cut the copy!

Proceed to cut the original blueprint into smaller patterns according to the design decided upon beforehand.

Afterwards, use each piece to make a slightly larger piece but of exactly the same shape. The science here is that for you to make a pattern of any design, you MUST use this method; it is a tried and tested system that is fail-proof. It is always a good idea to add about half of an inch all around each mini pattern while being very careful to retain the original shape and form.

The extra material on each mini pattern provides more room on the edges for use later on when you have to stitch the patterns; and when lasting.

If the chosen design dictates that there be holes or incisions on the upper, give special attention to each mini pattern that bears those peculiarities. This is important, as these peculiarities on the finished product would most likely be the focal point of admirers and critics alike.

In most cases, incisions and holes are added to the shoe purely for aesthetic reasons.

THE NEXT ACTION IS to find the materials that we will use to make the footwear. There are various kinds of leather materials; therefore, it is important to discuss them with your client before settling on a particular type. Explain the benefits and any known issues with each type of leather. Then **decide together** by balancing your professional recommendations, with her needs and preferences as the end-user.

When purchasing leather material, you will also need to buy other parts, perhaps at the same time. These include necessary items that will be used in preparing the seat of the shoes, the stiffs, the heels, the sole, the lining, nylon thread, rivets, nails, and/or screws.

Do not forget the strong adhesive that will be used throughout the process; this adhesive must be a very tough type and different from that used previously to create the mean pattern. The quality, and type of adhesive used, will ultimately determine the strength and also longevity of the final product.

The skills you demonstrate here will determine what the shoes will eventually look like.

That is why meticulous judgement is required at this stage because if the pattern were just a fraction of an inch larger or smaller, the footwear would not look appealing enough and may not fit well. Once again - Make sure that the blueprint sticks tightly to the custom Last before making any marks or incisions on it.

After making marks on this material, you will need to stop and use your trained imagination to determine what the shoes will look like at the end of production.

On this note: During my time at the Designing School, the fashion conception department used to offer whole modules on imagination alone. They viewed imagination as an important subject on its own merit; a discipline that prompts the designer to first visualise with his mind's eye what the final product would look like. If the custom designer's imagination is poor, he would be chasing shadows throughout; and might end up producing a pair of shoes that differ totally from that initially intended. Now - there is no harm in standing back from the blueprint after everything you have done so far. Do something else for a while and then return with fresh eyes to take a second look at what you are making.

THIS PROCESS, KNOWN in design/build as **mirroring**, allows the designer to isolate and correct any errors missed from his initial actions. But this can only be possible if he or she moved away from the studio, allowing his mind and eyes to focus on something else, before returning to the studio to resume his creation – *with a fresh mind and eyes.*

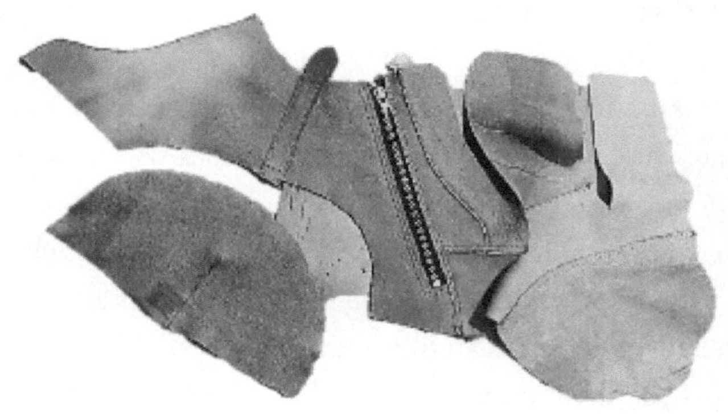

PREPARING THE UPPER

We now want to join the smaller pieces of patterns that we cut earlier together to make the upper part of the shoe. To do this, we need the initial blueprint created at the outset. This will guide us in putting the various pieces of patterns together to prepare the upper.

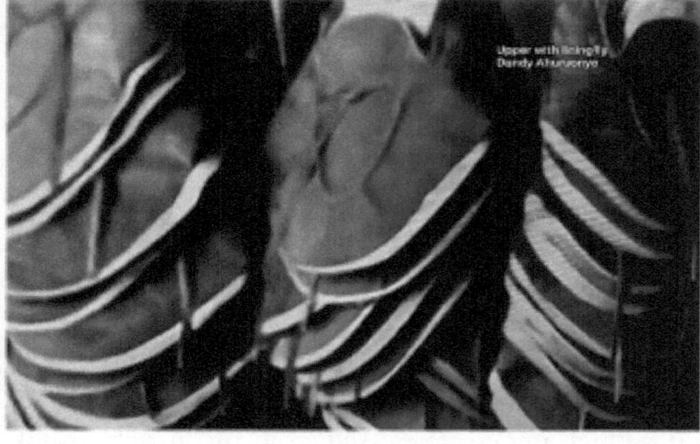

As a trial, use weak adhesive to join the mini patterns together just to get a fair idea of what the upper would look like. Next, use a strong adhesive to permanently join the pieces together.

Do this on top of the drawing that we did not cut up; the very first pattern that we made but did not enlarge. This is the vital Original!

Use that blueprint to make sure that the joining of the patterns is accurate. After joining them correctly with strong adhesive, it is time to sew the mini patterns together. Many custom designers use a needle and manually stitch them together; while others may choose to use a sewing machine. But it is worth noting that the type of stitching chosen will add to the quality and durability of the product.

The stitching plays an important role in complementing the overall design, but this may also depend on the actual type elected. Note also that in a case where the chosen design is a plain pair of cover shoes or open-fronted sandals, then you only need to sew the back of the upper where the stiff will eventually be attached.

In addition, some design types dictate that the pieces that form the upper cannot be sewn together. In this case, be very careful to use the strongest adhesive possible, or use industrial superglue to join the pieces of the upper together. Just watch out for excess adhesive oozing out of line and onto the other areas of the upper; this might mess up your product because often it might not be possible to remove this excess adhesive from the leather without inflicting noticeable damage to the material.

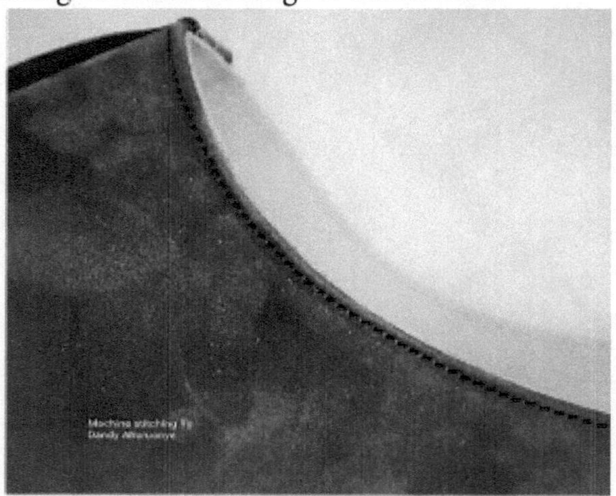

NEXT, WE NEED TO JOIN the lining to the upper. In most cases, the lining is prepared using plain leather or another similar material. At other times though, and depending on the design and the penchant of the customer, the lining material could be the same as the upper. This happens either with the plain material to be used or where it is to be cut into smaller bits and then joined to match up with the main upper material and design.

To stitch the lining onto the upper, hold both of them together, with the front or outer sides (sides that will eventually be exposed) facing each other. Then turn it inside out after stitching.

Maintain a steady hand if you opt to use a sewing machine and make sure the stitches run on top of the original marking made at the blueprint stage.

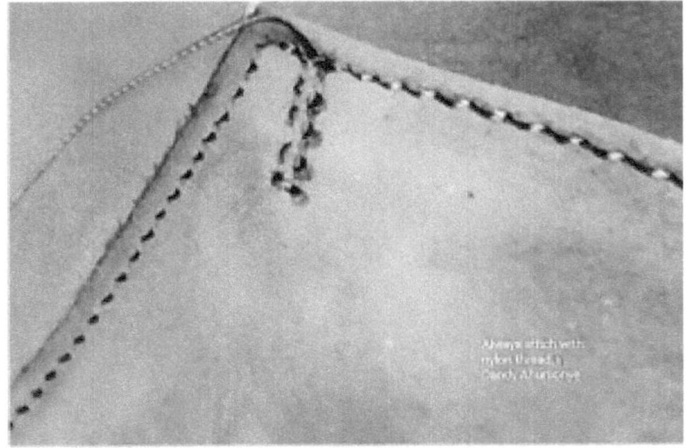

Nylon thread used on a good leather material ensures that the footwear boasts a robust quality.

CUT OUT THE EXCESS material afterwards, but leave about a quarter of an inch of extra material; otherwise, the stitches might come apart when under pressure.

IF POSSIBLE, USE NYLON thread for all sewing or stitching jobs that are to be completed.

Your focus now is on the rear of the upper. The line between the rear strap, the mid counter, and the lower counter rim towards the bottom end of the upper material is to be shaped into a slight 'C' form shape. This is to allow the rear stiff to be installed without much difficulty; therefore, follow this 'C' shape whilst stitching.

With both lining and upper now attached to one another to become one piece, divide the upper and lining into three parts using a marker. Then apply some adhesive onto the surface of the middle section of both the lining and the upper. Be very careful to avoid applying the gum around the front and rear demarcations, as these areas will eventually have to be hardened after receiving relevant stiffs.

When the adhesive has fully dried, carefully turn the upper and lining inside out now to expose the display surface areas. Use your fingers to cautiously form a rim or ridge along the stitch lines, so that the seam is pushed inside and held in place by the strong glue.

Once again - This requires maximum care, bearing in mind that the strong adhesive could damage the upper if you made a mistake and try to pull both upper and lining apart to carry out a correction. After attaching both successfully, our next task is to attach the stiffs at the rear of the upper material.

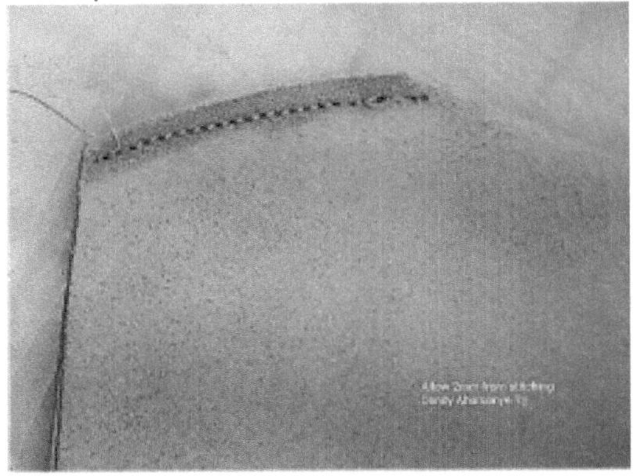

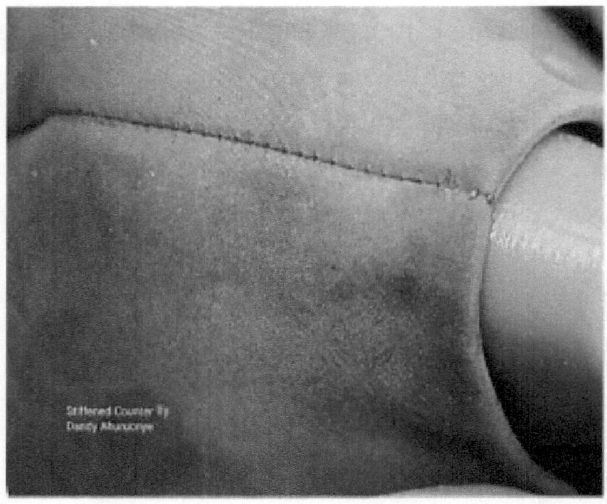
Stiffened Counter IIj
Dandy Ahuruonye

12: REAR STIFF

At the back of most covered shoes is the stiff. As the name suggests, this material hardens the rear of your shoes, making them fit firmly but comfortably around the protruding heels and sides of your feet. The slight, near-vertical or elongated 'C' shape of the rear of the upper we mentioned earlier will now play a critical role as it forms a mini cup or cradle for the ball of the foot. This ensures that the shoe will not come off on its own when walking or running. As in the case of the leather material, the stiffs come in various kinds - soft, short, long, sticker, plastic, leather, cardboard, metal, and the list goes on.

On occasions when the stiff is to be reattached after the designer had initially made a mistake, you may have to remove traces of the adhesive that had been applied. If not, there might be tiny bumps showing around the rear of the shoe later on, because of applying fresh adhesive on top of the previous application.

AS WE AIM TO USE STANDARD materials for our pair, if possible, we will settle for the soft plastic type of stiff. My reason for this choice is that the plastic brand is easier to attach to the rear of the upper leather material by hand. In addition, it does not peel apart if the designer makes a mistake and must remove or adjust the position of the stiff during attachment.

The easiest way to remove the initial adhesive is to dab inflammable liquid like kerosene on those specific areas and allow the area to dry properly before continuing. Inflammable liquids like kerosene or even petrol neutralise most types of adhesives without damaging the leather material.

However, it is important to note that once you apply this fuel to the leather material to remove previously applied adhesive, you must allow a considerable length of time for the material to shed the liquid through drying and evaporation. This may take about six to twenty-four hours, or even more, depending on the texture of the leather material you are working with. Hence, it is of immense benefit to avoid any mistakes when attaching stiffs; so, try to get it right the first time.

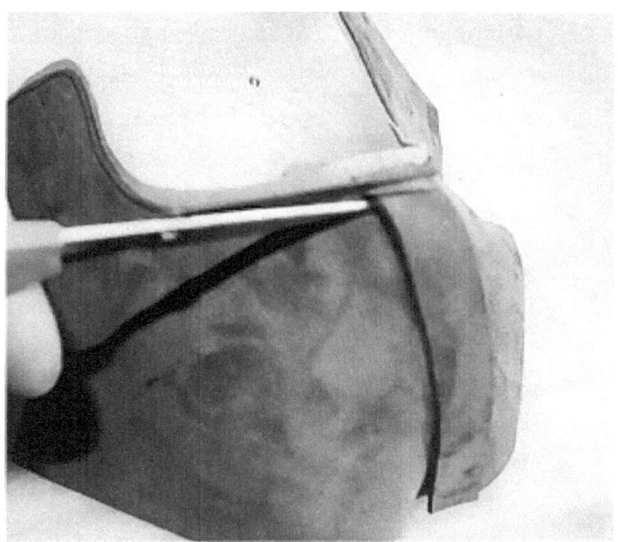

Apply some adhesive all over the stiff and do the same on the rear third of the upper that you marked out previously; allow the adhesive to dry properly. Cover both of them with a large cloth to prevent dust particles, sand, or other foreign objects - no matter how tiny - from resting on the surface of the adhesive.

With very steady hands, stick the top of the stiff to the top rim or counter of the inside of the upper, with the opposite end of the lining sticking upwards. Then use both the index finger and the thumb of your left hand to hold the top of the stiff while using the right hand to pull hard at the bottom edge of the upper to attach it to the other end of the stiff.

You must do this in a swift pull downwards action for maximum smoothness. With the middle of the stiff now attached partly to the upper, carefully pull one side of the material along the body of the stiff until they both firmly cling to each other. Do the same for the other side until the stiff becomes part of the upper. Then hold the top end of the lining that is sticking out and firmly pull it downwards.

After this downwards pull, try first to get the middle part to stick onto the stiff and then repeat the same process as in the upper's case; until the upper resembles something like a 'canoe.' Use the fingers to smooth out the entire body of this upper. Alternatively, hook it up on a knob or the knee and use force to stretch the upper until its rear end becomes very smooth.

Now we can see that a key part of our footwear is ready and can be used.

WE WILL USE A DIFFERENT kind of Stiff on the front end of covered shoes to make the front tip strong enough to protect the toes and add hardness and durability to the footwear.

The shoe front requires stiffs simply because we generally move or walk in the forward direction, and at speeds and in areas that put our toes in danger of striking objects that are lying static on the ground. Nonetheless, we must not confuse the roles of the rear and front stiffs.

Rear stiffs make it possible for the shoes to stay attached or stick to the hindfoot which forms the heel and ankle (ball of the foot), while the fronts stiff protect the forefoot (toes) from injury. Both stiffs also add to and maintain the desired shape of the footwear.

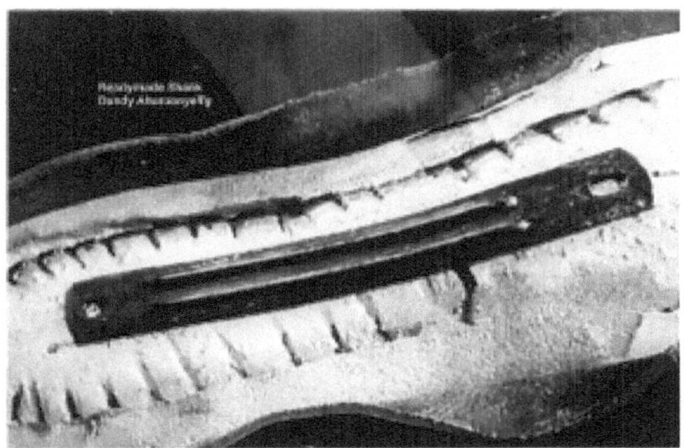
Readymade Shank
Dandy Abarionye'Ty

13: THE SHANK (METAL SHEET)

The shank is a key part of the supportive structure that combines the insole and outsole of footwear and runs underneath the midfoot (arch of the foot). The presence of a shank is central to the functionality of the shoe as it takes on much of the load incurred by the wearer's feet and lower leg while walking (especially when going uphill).

The shank is therefore a significant provider of support to the foot and also contributes to the general form and elegance of a shoe.

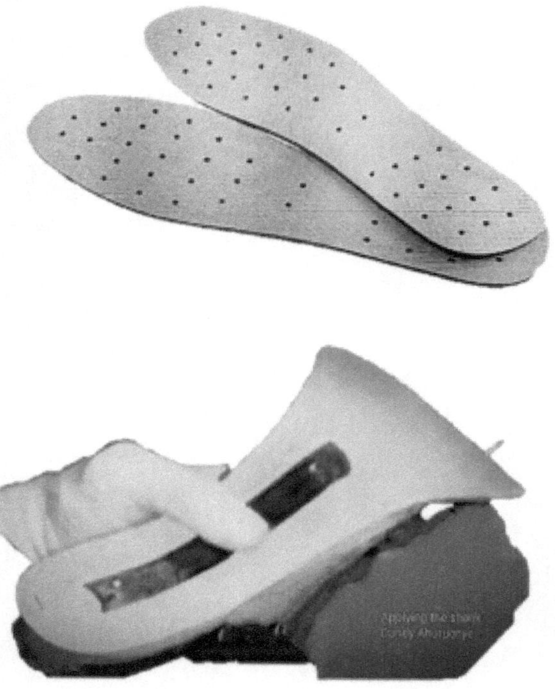

The most durable shanks are made of tough metal material and are inserted between the insole and outsole or the midfoot part of the shoe. Its range extends from the middle of the heel (the hindfoot) to the beginning of the front of the foot (the forefoot). Besides supporting and guiding the foot, the shank preserves the shoe's form.

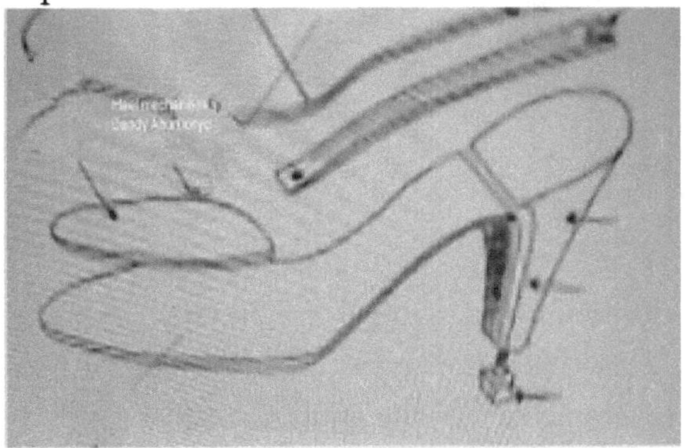

Depending on the shape and size of the customer's feet, the metal sheet can measure between 7 to 10 centimetres; and 1- 2 centimetres in width. This metal rod must be flat and lies in the hollow created by the welt and the insole, between the heel and the ball of the foot. You must shape the metal material to fit the curve of the sole and steady the foot during wear; while simultaneously preventing the heel from wobbling.

Because of the central role the shanks play in a shoe, we apply them to the middle (inside) of the shoe seat, mostly to enforce a shape, but also to determine the height of the product. In most cases, they also determine how steep or flat the shoe will become, except where the Seat or sole is prefabricated.

This is usually the case when the Seat is made of glass, iron, aluminium, bones, or wood.

In such cases, we assume that the Seat material is tough enough on its own, and so would not require the application of an external shank.

For the pair we are making, we will use an all-state stainless metal shank that is ultra-tough. The shanks can be hand-forged into the desired shape and steepness, using a metal tool. It is possible to purchase shanks that are already cut into desired width, length, and thickness; then you only have to shape it into your required steepness. Assuming this is not the case, then you would have to fabricate your shanks to meet your specific needs.

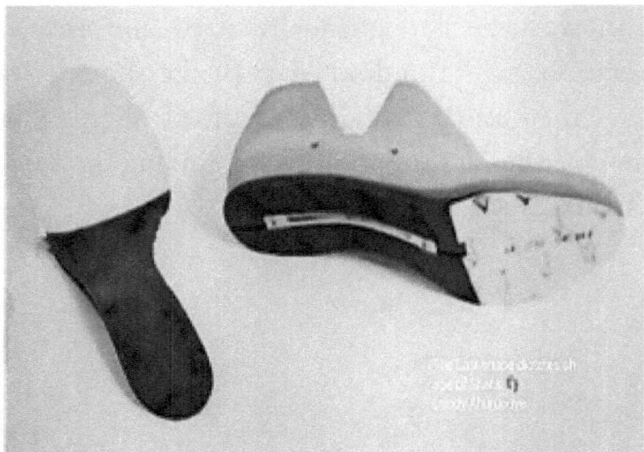

Beforehand, go to your local scrapyard, and select a durable piece of metal that is also very lightweight. Take this metal sheet to a blacksmith for cutting and give him the required measurement(s) of the shanks.

Ask the blacksmith to drill two holes at the rear end of each shank. The first hole should be approximately half an inch from the rear edge; the second hole should be another half inch from the first.

After the cutting and the drilling of holes, you can now attempt to forge them into your desired shape or form. To do this, get a kerosene or gas stove, a medium-sized hammer, a pair of large pliers, a pair of protective gloves and goggles, and a prefabricated heavy metal-forge base (mini smithy). If it is not possible to secure such a tool, look for an alternative in the form of a cast-iron (large or small) cobbler shoe mould or stand (anvil).

Now heat the shank on the stove until it becomes red hot, and at a temperature where it becomes easier to shape by forging. Hold it securely in place using the pair of pliers as tongs; the same way a workpiece is held on the smithy's anvil while the smith works it with a forge hammer. Then apply force using the hammer until you achieve the required shape.

For your safety, it is of utmost importance that you grip firmly and securely on the shank using the long pliers. If the shank flies off your grip, it may cause a serious accident for you or anyone nearby; it could also damage equipment or other items in the workshop.

Since we are using stainless steel for our pair, there is no need to worry about rust and stuff like that. However, in the event that the stainless brand is not available, then you can just use an ordinary sheet of metal. In this case, be sure to use coarse sandpaper to remove rust from the shank before applying adhesive.

***FIRE IS USED TO FORGE** a blade of steel shank; because when the steel blade is heated and cooled, the shank becomes stronger and serves a better purpose.*

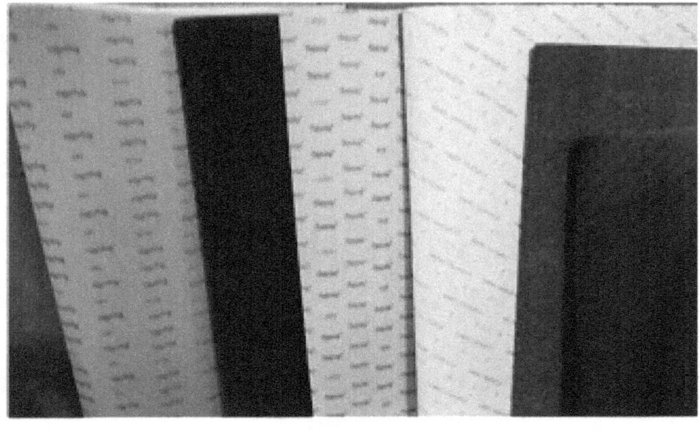

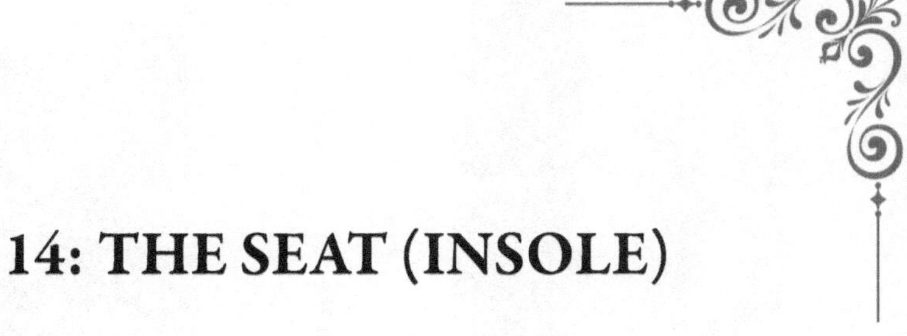

14: THE SEAT (INSOLE)

The shoe sole is divided into three principal parts: the insole, outsole and midsole. The insole cradles and bolsters the foot. This shoe seat is the most important part of footwear, mainly because it carries the entire weight of the person wearing it. Therefore, the Seat must be very tough, durable, and flexible; while also being lightweight and shock-absorbing.

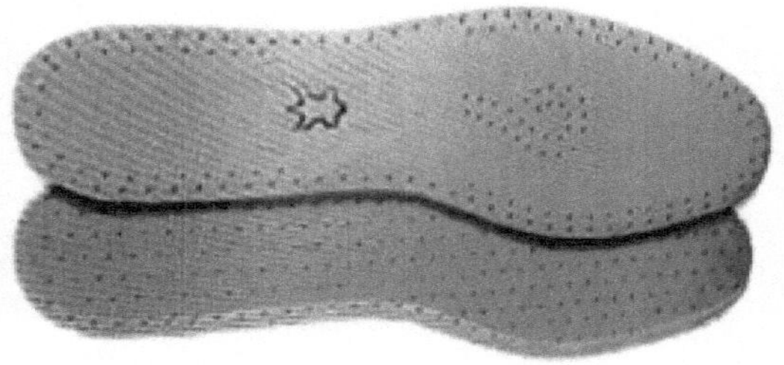

The insole of the shoe is the first layer of the sole. It is directly beneath the foot and is designed to attach to the upper of the shoe. Some specialists referred to the insole as the footbed of the shoe. As the name suggests, the Seat should be structured and contoured to serve as a framework for the foot to balance on. Because of advances in science and technology, today we can construct some insoles with anti-microbial chemicals that help keep the shoe free from foul smells. We can also build shoes worn in less temperate parts of the world with some types of insulated footbeds.

The shoe sole must be designed in such a way that it gives the shoe vast durability that withstands being scraped on the ground countless times. Hence, the sole is simply the bottom or ground end of the shoe. Soles are unpretentious parts made using one layer of material made from natural rubber, leather, polyurethane and PVC compounds. However, master artisans constructing soles using multiple layers is an advanced way to double up their durability and their function.

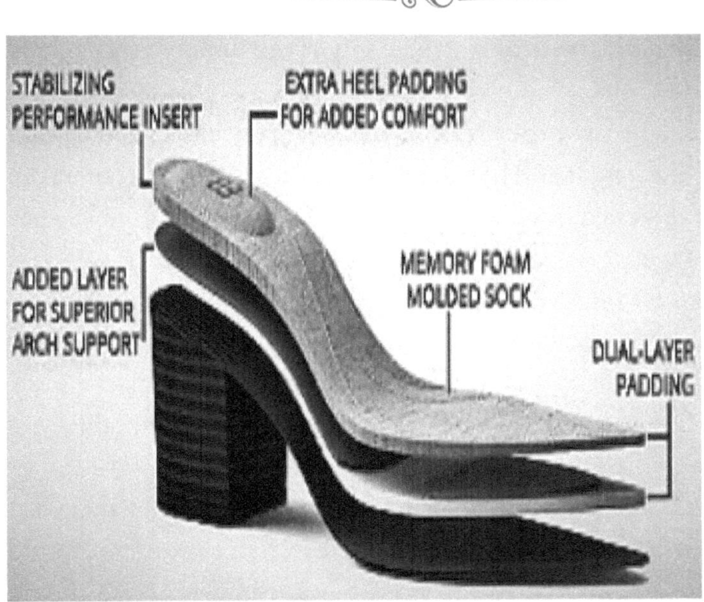

OTHER KINDS OF MATERIAL can also be effective in preparing seats for footwear. Today, it is commonplace to see shoe insoles made of vinyl, ethylene, cardboard, paper, leather, plastic, glass, metal, wood, aluminium, and even bones. The reason for this long list of materials is that the Seat must be very tough for it to withstand the stress and hardship it will undergo throughout the lifetime of the shoe.

As most shoemakers use the insole to achieve many aims like - enforcing a shape, determine the height and how steep or flat the shoe will become, the seat or insole must be designed in such a manner to last as long as other key parts of the shoe; if not longer.

Take, for example, an everyday pair of shoes worn for up to three years. Assume you walk for three kilometres a day wearing this; and since there are approximately 1600 steps in a kilometre, this user may have taken nearly two million steps in that period. This statistic illustrates why the durability of the Seat cannot be overemphasised.

The cobbler may repair most other parts of a shoe, but not the Seat. The Seat is the spine or backbone of the shoe, therefore, in most cases, it would not be possible to remove the Seat to carry out a repair intervention. Unless in a case where the cobbler decides to tear apart the footwear and rebuild it from scratch. For the pair we are looking to make, we will use standard leather fibre material to build its Seat.

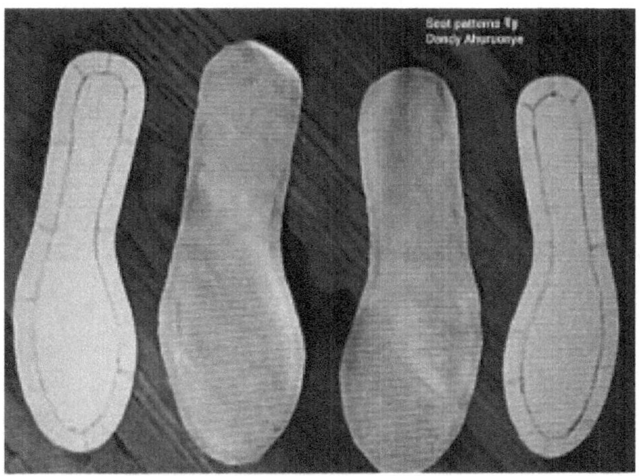

PREPARING THE SEAT

Mark out a pattern from the bottom part of the Last on a piece of paper or cardboard and cut it out, we will use this as the main pattern for the Seat. To do this, place the Last in the middle of the blueprint of one of her feet and, using a marker of unique colour, impress a mark of the bottom of the Last onto the middle of the blueprint. You immediately notice that the mark from the Last is slightly smaller and sits inside the blueprint. This is normal since the idea is to make the footwear to be smaller than the foot to such an extent for it to grip and remain attached to the foot when she puts on the shoe.

I recommend that leather fibre material be used to prepare the Seat since this type of material is very tough and yet lightweight; it also breathes, allowing the inside of the shoe to keep fresh and reduce moisture and unpleasant odour.

Place the fibre on a flat surface, place the custom-made Last on the material, then use a fine ballpoint marker or pen to mark out an exact pattern of the sole of the Last. When doing this, make sure that the Last does not move!

Using a mid-sized sharp pair of scissors, accurately cut out this pattern along the marked lines. Use a small nail (tack), or weak adhesive, to attach this pattern on the bottom of the Last just to be sure it is exactly of the same shape and size as the Last. Once you are certain that the pattern perfectly matches the Last, remove it from the Last and use it to mark out four copies from the fibre material. When cutting the patterns, cut about half a millimetre on the inside from the ballpoint pen mark. Now you have five copies, use the four to proceed, and keep the fifth safe as a blueprint in the event of damage or loss of the Seat(s). Using the four odds, apply strong adhesive on opposite surfaces of each pair. Bear in mind that these are viewed as 'odds' and therefore should be treated as opposites of each other at all times.

Apply adhesive all over the shanks and allow all six items to dry.

Place the shank in the middle of one of the fibre materials about half an inch from the rear edge; use your fingers, or a plastic hammer to press it firmly onto the Seat until fully bonded. Then place the middle of the other odd onto the opposite surface of the shank.

The two sheets must face each other at a perfectly matched angle, with the shank now installed in the middle. At this stage, we can shape the Seat into various forms depending on the shoes' design; and whether the shoes will be flat, high-heeled, short-heeled, or medium.

The shanks must reflect the height of the heels we are to use. As explained in the previous section, to adjust the shape of the shanks you can use a shank bender by placing the shanks in the middle of the bender and applying pressure on the point you want to depress or lift, until the required shape and tilt have been achieved.

If you must reshape the shank that's already attached to the fibre, utmost care must be observed. Otherwise, the Seat and fibre might be perforated and therefore damaged.

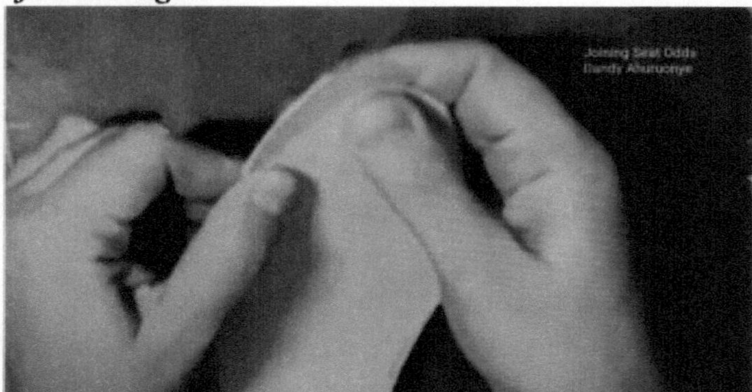

First, push down firmly to close the gap between the two sheets of fibre at the rear end of the shanks, this will create a cup-like shallow hollow in the middle of the insole with the shank also creating a steep rise-and-fall shape that looks like a winding 'S.'

Now hold the Seat in an elongated manner by pressing the heel end to your sternum; with the eight fingers underneath and the thumbs on top.

As you push down your thumbs, pull your fingers upwards and sideways, this will create a slight gutter-like V shape in the middle of the Seat. Use a plastic hammer to press down the rest of the Seat so that the two sheets form one item with the shank now discernible, but invisible.

BY APPLYING PRESSURE on the Seat in the making, and by pushing the middle part downwards and pushing the sides upwards, the insole will now look a bit like a miniature boat. The middle part must be hollow enough to allow the foot to sit comfortably on it.

There must be no gaps between the sheets of fibre and the shank, hence the need to use a plastic hammer to apply a gentle but firm force until you achieve the required full bonding. At this point, hold up the Seat across

your face with both hands, at eye level.

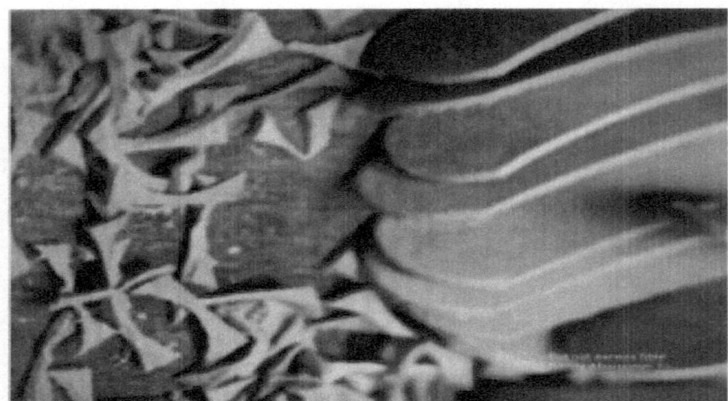

The rear part of the Seat should now look somewhat like a semi-flat surface, while the middle descends sharply down into the hollow in the middle. The final third of the Seat towards the front should remain flat - from the hollow - to the pointing front end.

Carefully run the sharp blade of your channel knife along the edges of the Seat from a slanted angle to maintain the 'V' shape; otherwise, you can also use a smoothing machine to achieve the same result.

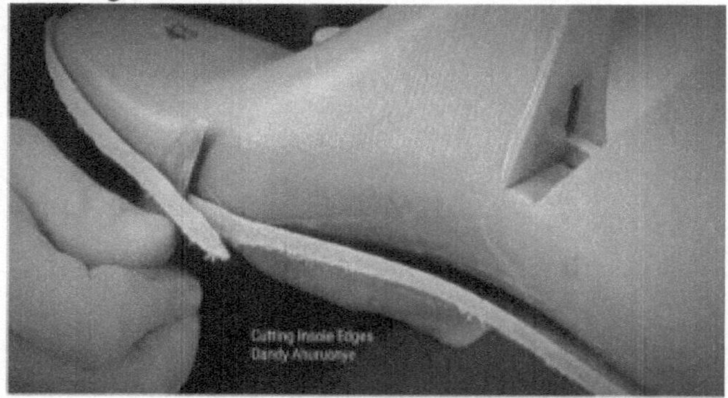

BE EXTREMELY CAREFUL while doing this, as even the slightest mistake at this point will ultimately alter the shape and the appearance of the final product. Also, using a channel knife can be dangerous if one is distracted in any way.

TAKE ONE LAST LOOK at the Seat to be certain there are no rough spots or edges. The Seat must be perfect for the shoe to look good when finished.

With the Seat and upper ready for use, our attention will now shift to the heels and the sole (outsole).

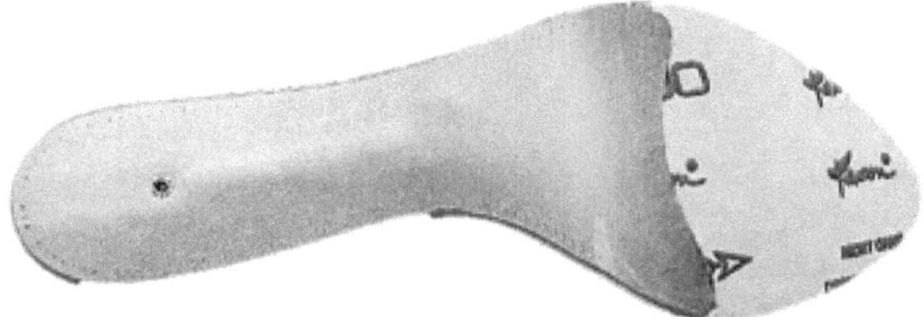

Some masters may also use a metal file to smoothen the edges of the Seat manually.

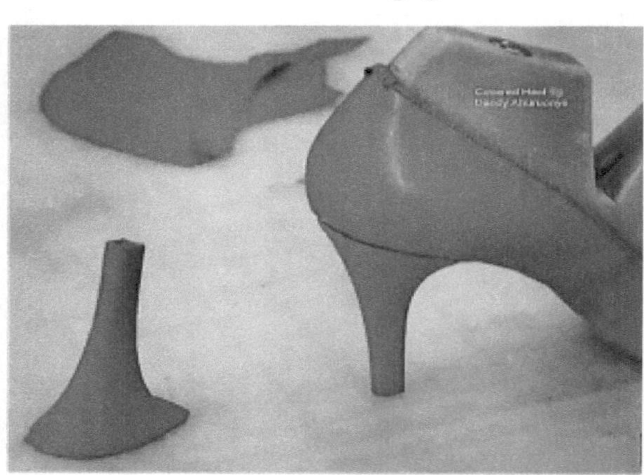

15: THE HEEL

The heel of a shoe is an independent piece of material that raises the rearmost part of the shoe. Here is a list of the names of heel parts:

Heel Tip - The narrow tip of a shoe with a high heel (Top Piece).

Heel Breast - The area of the heel that faces the shoe front, typically below the arch area of the foot.

Heel Seat - The part of the heel attached to the sole of a shoe.

Top Piece - The area of the heel that contacts the ground.

A DESIGNING STUDENT might ask why we refer to the tip of the shoe heel as the 'Top Piece.' This is a technical jargon or industry term; the reason for this verbiage is that when a shoe is being constructed, you can almost always install the heel on the shoe while the shoe is upturned. In that case, the bottommost part of the heel now becomes the highest point (during the shoe assembly process).

In some parts of the world, most heels used in making footwear are readymade. So, it is just a case of choosing a suitable pair at the shoe parts dealership; but if you are designing a bespoke pair of shoes, then you must prepare the heels you are going to use.

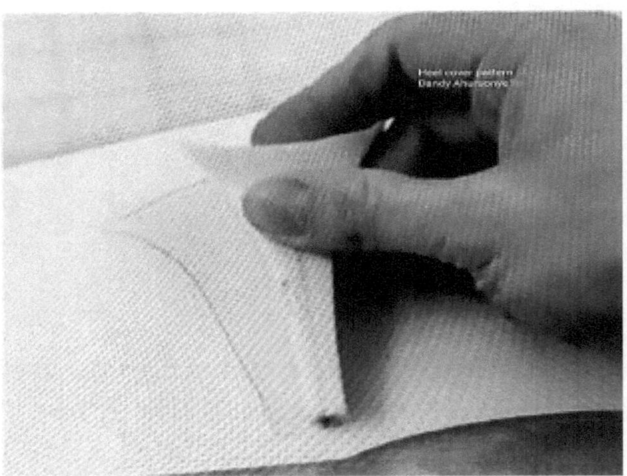

SHOE HEELS CAN BE MADE from every kind of material - wood, iron, aluminium, bones, concrete, rubber, plastic, leather, cardboard. The list is endless. It is possible to see these items in most types of shoes.

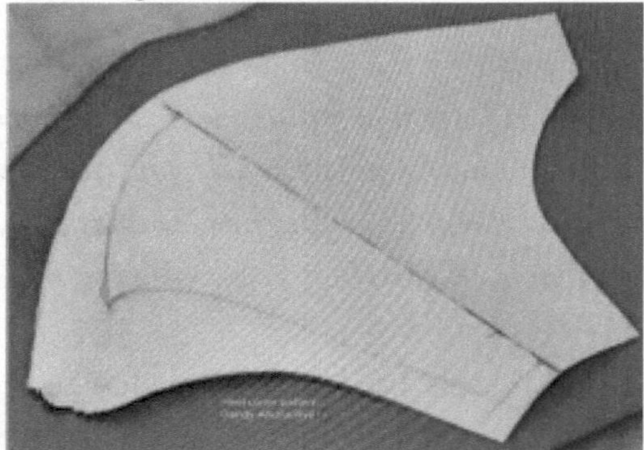

However, some designs are made in such a notoriously subtle manner that the heel may not become obvious; an example being some of Dr Scholl's brands of slippers, flat shoes, or sandals.

Like the Seat, the quality and durability of the heel are crucial to the overall strength of the footwear. Some heels are flat, spherical, pointed, and squared. You can find all kinds of shapes and sizes of heels depending on the type of shoe you want to get. From my perspective, the chosen design, and the preferences of the end-user, should decide the shape, size, and appearance of the heel.

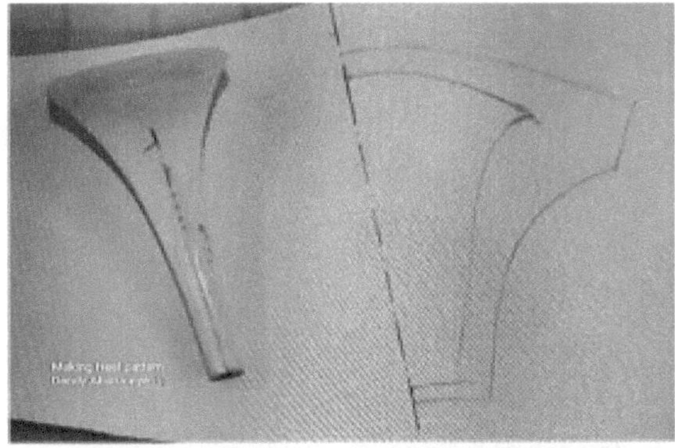

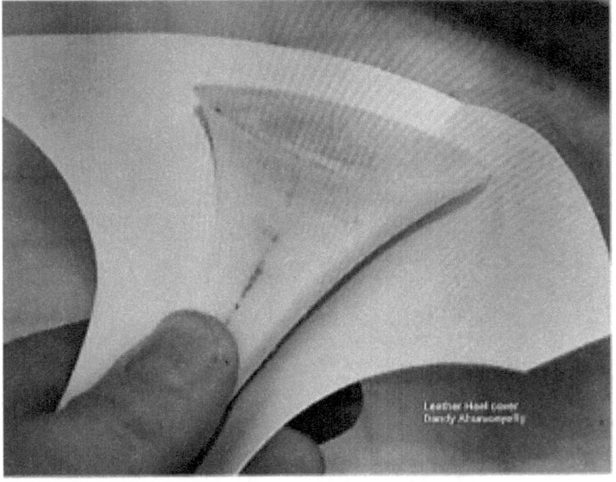

AS WE HAVE NOTED ALREADY, these are to be agreed upon during the conception stage of the footwear. We must construct the chosen heel with highly durable material. It is also important that the heels be very lightweight since the lighter the shoe is, the better for the end-user.

For our pair we will use an industrial pair of heels that are made of aluminium material; this type is very durable and yet lightweight.

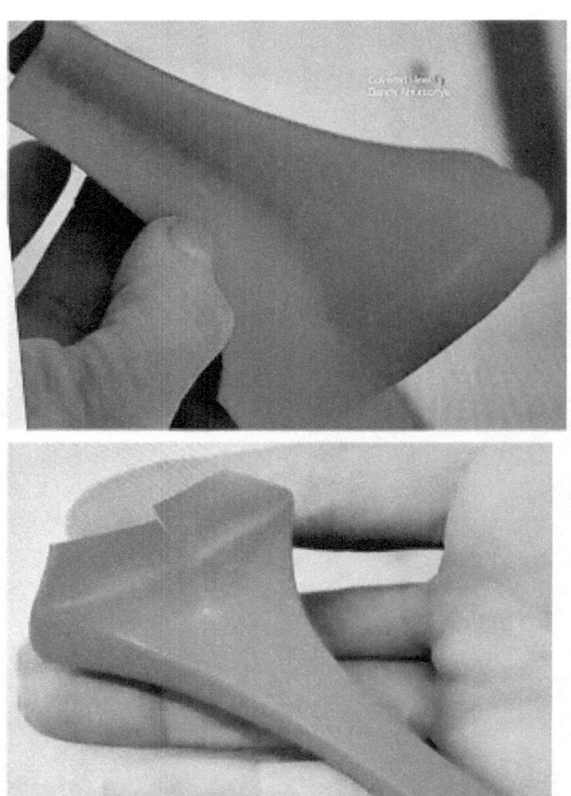

You can either spray the heel with paint to match the colour of the leather material, or cover it with the same material as the upper for a full-colour match. There are advantages and disadvantages to choosing either type of heel.

FOR THE SPRAYED HEEL, the advantage is that the pointing tip wears normally while the disadvantage is that it is almost impossible to find a paint that matches 100% with the colour of the main leather material used for the upper.

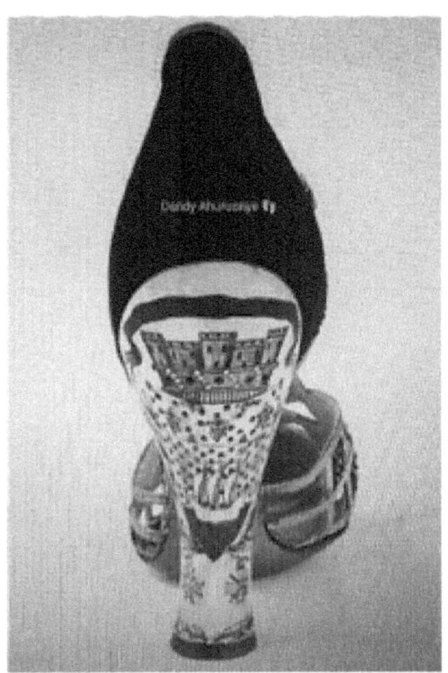

For the heel folded with the leather material, you gain 100% colour match; but the downside is that - as you continue to use the shoe, the material will peel and show scratches and dents because of the knocks and bangs that are inevitable on the ground.

As well, the material on the pointing tip of the heel may come off because of atmospheric pressure. When this happens, it will form a hairy-looking mess at the top piece of the heels. For our pair, we will use the spray-painted heel.

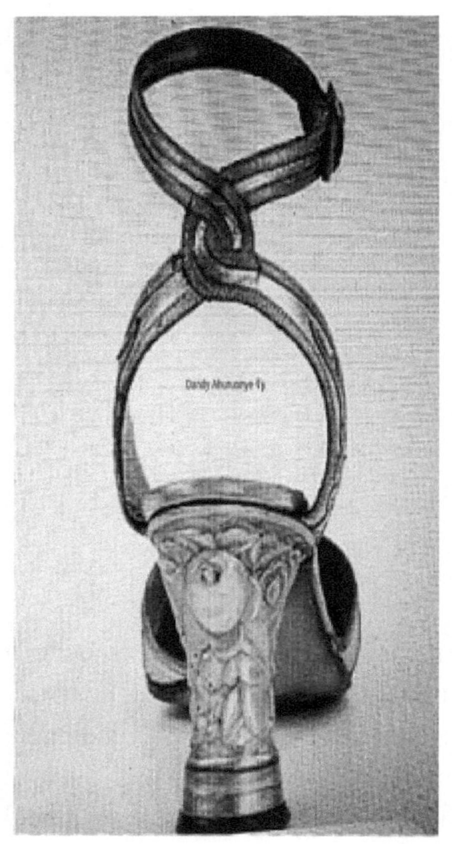
Dandy Ahuruonye Fy

16: THE SOLE

While deciding what shoes to purchase, lots of people do not pause and give serious consideration to the sole of the footwear they choose. These people do not realise that wearing the wrong type of shoes on a particular surface can hurt their feet; and may also damage the shoes. Nonetheless, most shoe sole manufacturers today make certain that all soles they produce provide some measure of grip.

These are among the common sole types that are available in many parts of the world today:

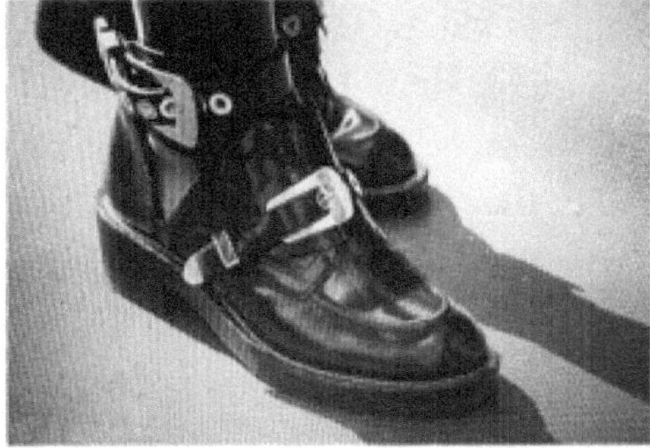

Rubber soles

Rubber soles are made of organic, and sometimes recycled rubber. Such materials are waterproof, flexible, and durable. They can withstand the rigours of everyday use by resisting wear and tear; they can also be adapted to suit different type of shoe styles.

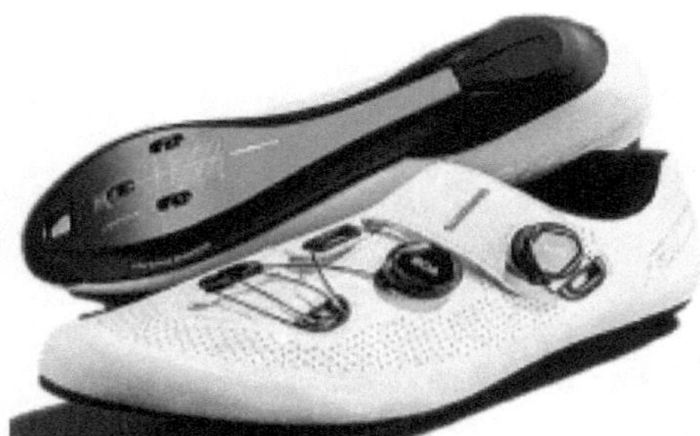

Lugged soles

These soles are weather-resistant; usually, they are heavy soles and can be used in making various utility boots. They are typically made with rubber materials; and are famous for providing a great grip on the terrain. Some people nickname them *the commando soles* due to their being ideal for rough and slippery ground, or places where your feet require extra protection, such as work zones. On the downside, they require regular cleaning because they tend to accumulate dirt between the lugs; hence their name.

Christy soles

The Christy sole is a reliable lightweight product that provides great traction and has a reputation for a stable grip. However, their defining characteristic is that they have no defined heel. They're made of blown-up rubber material and have a ripple pattern. They're artistically pleasing to the eye, and therefore many see them as a very ideal addition to the wardrobe.

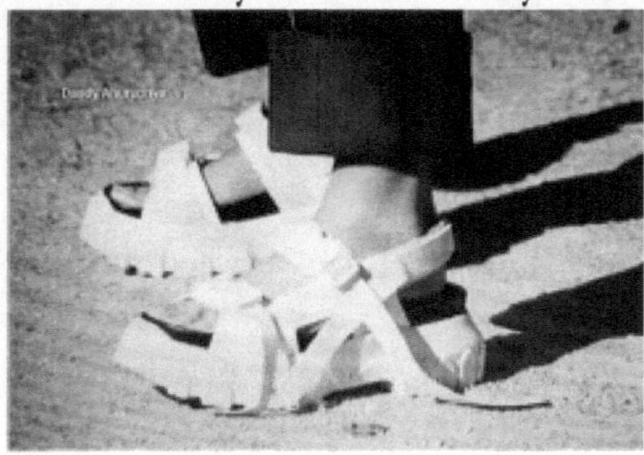

THEY ARE NOT AS ROBUST *as lugged soles when it comes to facing the challenges of rough terrain.*

CAMP SOLES

Camp soles are made of rubber, are lightweight and waterproof, but still deliver great traction. Despite being originally designed for casual footwear, we often find camp soles on loafers, Moccasins, and some types of slippers.

I have only highlighted some mainstream soles; however, there are many other types of soles that are not included in this book.

The sole links up into or onto the heel as both work in unison to form the so-called **Ground Forces** of the shoe. On a serious note, these two are among the most important parts of the shoe, protecting the feet from various dangers, hazards, and elements.

Some of these dangers are very obvious and may include sharp objects, rough surfaces, wet surroundings, floods, heat, cold, and other perils that otherwise might harm your feet.

IN SOME DESIGNS, THE heel may not be obvious, especially where the shoe has prominent soles instead. Such ones are usually made of rubber, wood, cardboard, bones, or a combination of several other materials.

ONCE AGAIN, THE EMPHASIS is on the quality, durability, and weight of the sole. Shoes with soles are mostly flat or semi-flat designs, but on occasions, the design may incorporate both heel and sole in a prefabricated mould. Soled shoes are mainly walking shoes because of their general comfortability and flatness.

The designs of some soles allow them to withstand slippery or oily surfaces. We refer to these as - anti-slip soles; they mostly cost more than normal soles because they are made of special nylon material.

Soles made only of leather material is the easiest to work with; it is also the most beautiful to behold. However, it is the softest and therefore does not last long in tropical environments, or with heavy use. Some other types of soles can be made from a combination of fibre and special plastic material known as Nora or etch leather.

Prefabricated Industrial Nora Soles

SUPERIOR RAW SHEET of Nora is the type we will use for our pair because this is among the most popular and widely used types of sole. It lasts longer even though it weighs slightly more than some other materials. The Nora material comes in a flat form and various thicknesses.

To prepare a pair of Nora soles manually, first, make a pattern using any kind of thick paper or cardboard. To get an accurate pattern, use the Seat pattern and mark out a copy on the cardboard. On this copy, place the heel at the beginning and use a pen with a large ballpoint to draw a line at the front of the heel. With the same pen, draw a clean, slight C-shaped line from the marking in front of the heel to about an inch before the beginning of the hollow part of the Seat.

The gap from the C-shaped line to the edges on both sides of the Seat should be approximately 1/3 of an inch. Cut off this bit along the C line from the end of the heels to the point just before the start of the hollow descent. The C lines should both be facing outwards.

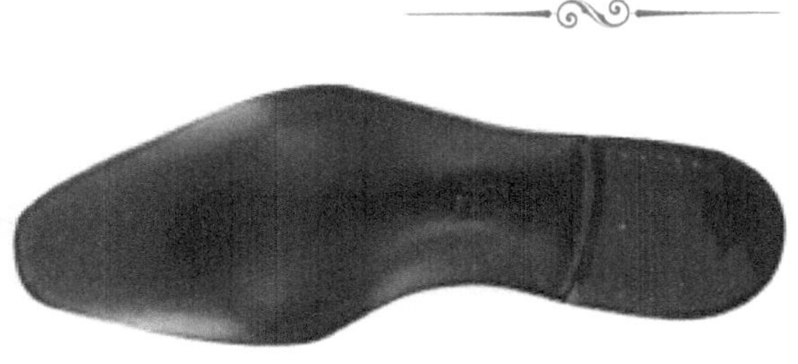

PLACE THIS PATTERN on the blueprint of the Seat, the fronts of both the Seat and sole patterns should be of the same size at the front from the hollow area to the front end.

However, from the end of the shank just before the hollow up towards the heel, the sole must be slightly smaller than the Seat. The reduction should begin with about 1mm from around the end of the shank to about 2 or 3mm at the front of the heel.

It is around this section of the sole that the 'C' shape mentioned earlier is applied.

Once the sole pattern is ready, then get a sheet of Nora material and mark out a pair of soles. As usual, we prepare everything regarding shoes in pairs as each item poses as an odd or opposite of the other.

When marking out parts; turn the pattern over every other time.

Use the channel knife to smooth out the edges carefully and then use a miniature paintbrush (or cotton bud) to apply a touch of permanent gloss along the rim of the Nora sole to make the edges shine a bit while making sure the gloss paint does not get on the surfaces. Preparing the Nora sole is probably the simplest, and the easiest step in shoe construction. The parts are then fitted and stitched together according to the chosen design.

There are other types of a sole that you can also use, especially when you are building gents' shoes or booths; here is a list of some of them, and their characteristics:

Counter

A reinforced piece of cardboard, leather, plastic, a mixture of some or all of these, or other strong but flexible material that is installed between the shoe lining and the upper at the rear of the shoe, immediately above the heel or rear sole, as with a flat shoe. Because it sits where the lining and outer shaft meet at the rear of the shoe, the Counter serves as a continuation of the heel, gripping the foot in place within the shoe. Thus, the purpose of the counter is mostly to reinforce the rear and, therefore, support the heel of the foot. It also helps retain the shape of the shoe. In other instances, the Heel Counter may refer to the external decoration around the rear of a shoe.

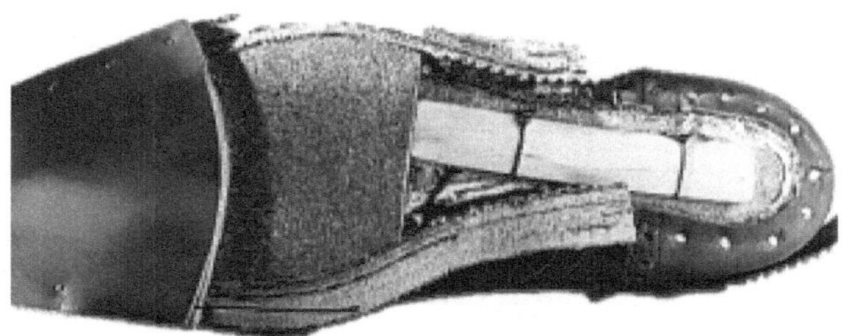

Filler

An elastic material such as cork or felt used to fill the hollow between the insole and the midsole. We know this material as the Filler. Over time, the filler is moulded by the pressure and warmth of the wearer's foot as well as by his or her weight distribution across the foot. This eventually leads to the formation of an individual footbed. At the same time, the filler muffles the wearer's tread and protects his foot from environmental elements like cold and heat.

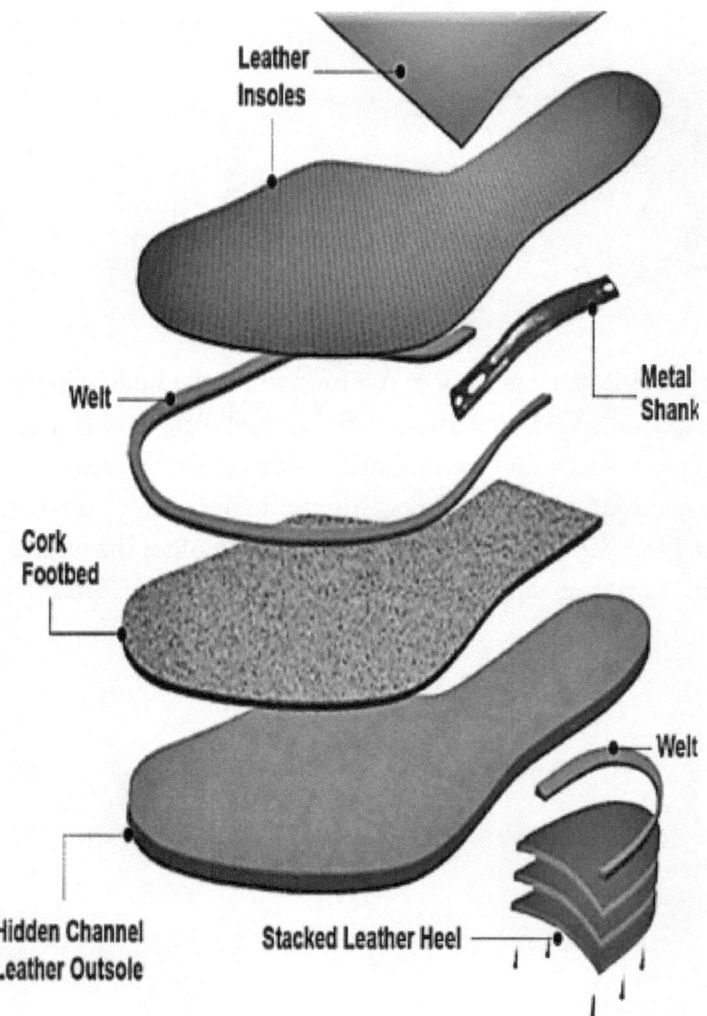

Leather
Insoles
Welt
Metal
Shank
Cork
Footbed
Welt
Hidden Channel
Leather Outsole
Stacked Leather Heel

Insole Lining

A soft leather layer that extends from the toe of the shoe to the heel. The foot normally rests upon the insole—as a result, the insole significantly influences wearing comfort and the way the foot feels inside the shoe. Because of this, the insole must be made using first-class, vegetable-tanned cowhide.

Outsole

The bottommost sole layer of the shoe, similar to Nora Soles. Elegant models feature a sole that is about 5 millimetres thick. The outsole makes direct contact with the ground when the shoe is in use. The outsole is usually made of vegetable oak or pit-tanned leather, which is particularly abrasion-resistant and waterproof. The outsoles used on some of the more affordable shoes, though, can also be made of rubber, synthetic material, Nora material, or wood.

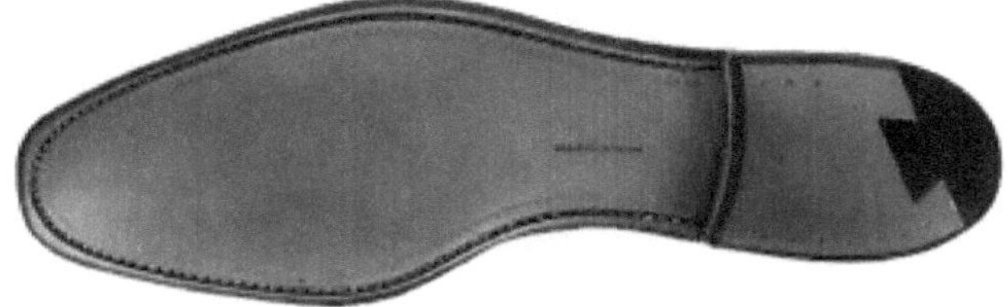

Mid outsole

A soft leather cover that stretches over the insole. On the side facing the foot, the mid-outsole ought to be abrasion-free, discolouration-resistant, and perspiration-resistant. The length of the mid-outsole varies by shoe type — it can cover the entire length, three-quarters of the length, or even a mere quarter of the length of the insole.

Heel tip

A piece of oak-pit-tanned leather that is cut out from the heel to ensure heel stability.

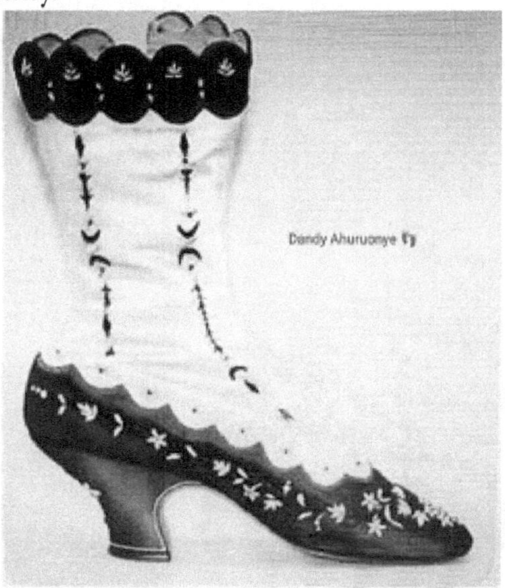

Top lift

The uppermost leather layer of the heel which comes directly in contact with the ground is known as the top lift. This part of the bottommost section of the shoe which, as we noted earlier, can also be referred to as the 'Top Piece.' It is made of reinforced plastic, metal, bone, or leather. It often features an abrasion-resistant rough edge. Sometimes, the top lift is made entirely of rubber or aluminium nail.

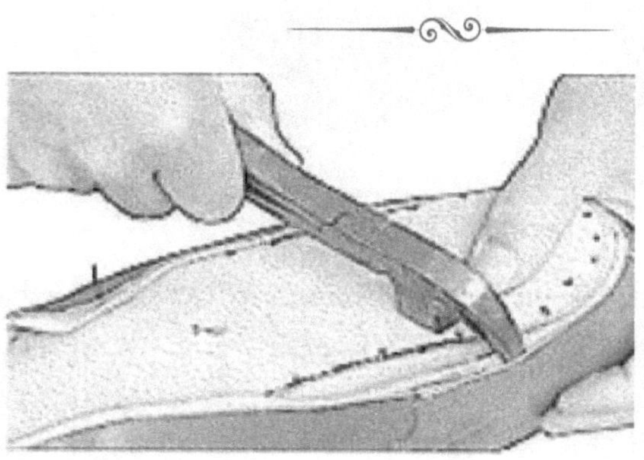

17: LASTING: QUICK SUMMARY

THE LASTING PROCESS or *Lasting* is a process that attaches and anchors the upper to the Seat first, with several tiny nails or tacks.

Next, the shoemaker will hammer the firm but flexible sole into the desired shape before the heel lifts are attached, together with the outsole that was nailed down to the lifts, this time using strong glue. The finishing technique involved lots of manual scraping, rasping, smoothing, parting, blacking, and burnishing the top lines of the heels and soles. Sometimes, the leather upper may require similar attention.

Before the shoe is removed from the last, the craftsman will need to scrape, sand-paper, and burnish the soles. Finally, he will withdraw the lasts, clean out or file down any pins that are sticking out and anything else which may be out of place.

SHOEMAKING IS NOT JUST about the making up of the upper or lasting. If you want to be free, you need to know how to create patterns from nothing otherwise; you are going to be making the same shoe repeatedly with no way to vary it.

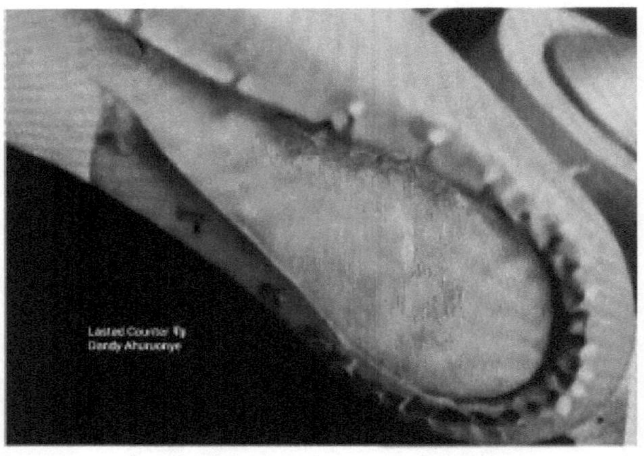

LASTING THE BACK

To pull the back down once the front is Lasted, remove the nail holding the upper on to the last and Insole, around the heel area. With the pincers, tug at the lining, working from the inside waist to the outside waist or vice versa; with special emphasis at the very back of the Seat. This is to take out any wrinkles and stop the lining from being caught up when the upper and lining and stiffener are gripped and pulled down together. For this bit of Lasting, the pincers cannot push the upper away from the last very far, and at this point, the lasting becomes quite difficult.

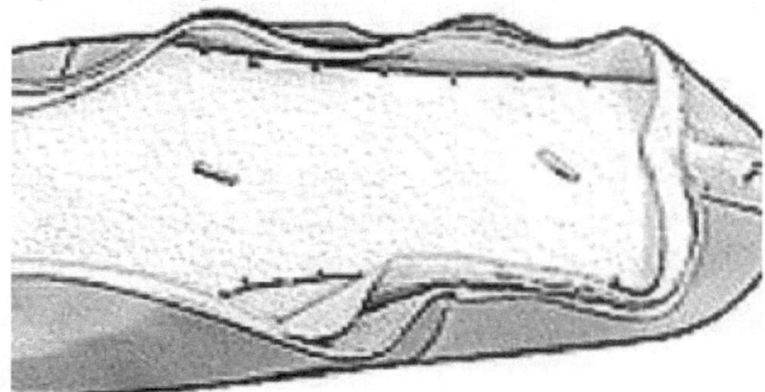

Make sure that the lining and stiffener come together with the upper, or they will smear gum paste onto the last and wrinkle at the top of the last, making it difficult to pull over; they could even leave a lump inside the topline.

Use the leverage of the pincers to pull the bottom of the upper downwards to provide material to wrap under the insole, while at the same time making sure that the topline clears the top of the Last by pushing it with the fingers of your free hand.

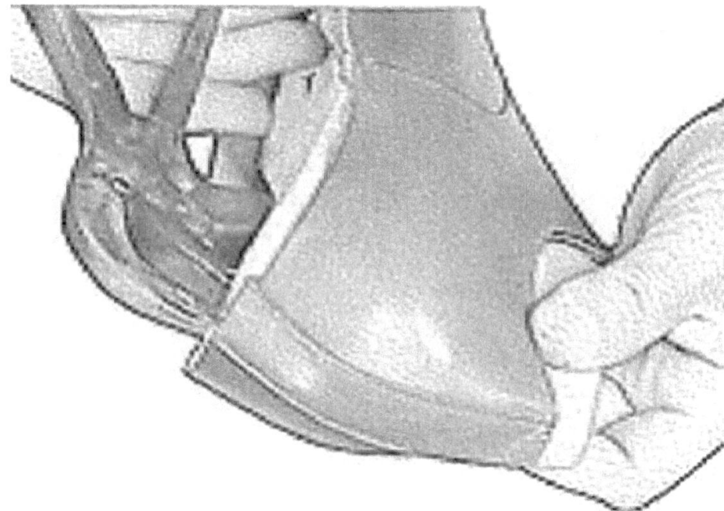

The lining may have to be pulled a bit more here to clear it at the top of the last and if it is needed, the upper may be pushed back up again to allow the lining to be straightened before pulling it down once again. Make sure that the insole does not get curled up with the lining because both of them have received some adhesive and so will be very sticky.

When the topline has been pulled down to the rear height mark, put a heavy nail through the upper, just down from the Topline, so that when any more pulling is done, the top will stay right on the line. Tug the upper, lining, and stiffener under the last at the rear seam, and fix it to the insole with a thin nail or tack.

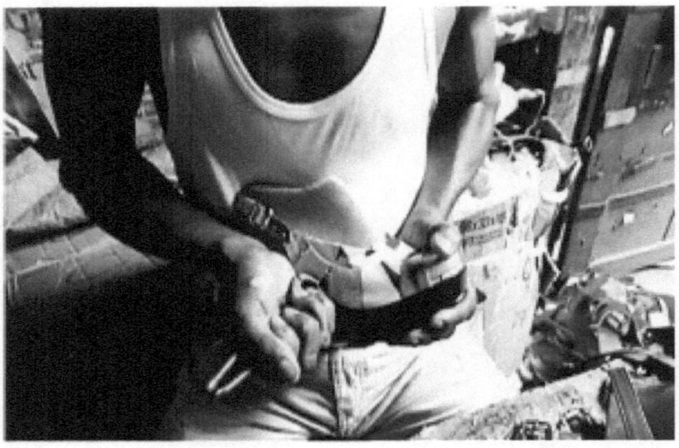

THE STIFFENER MUST come over the edge of the insole to be fixed, so it will set and provide rigidity to the back of the shoe. If it doesn't, then the upper will not be held in place at the feather edge and might collapse at that point, or later which would cause serious problems. If this happens, the stiffener would become useless, so always check this before moving on.

THE NEXT TWO PULLS using the pincers are made at right angles to the edge of the Last in the area that the front of a heel would come to rest on; which is about ½ way down the Seat area from the back of the Last.

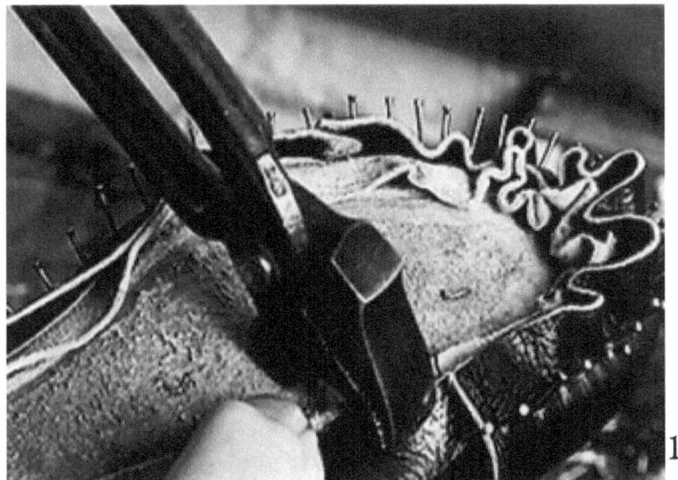

1.	http://oldleathershoe.com/
wordpress/?attachment_id=1385

18: DETAILED LASTING PROCESS

We will start by first applying some strong adhesive along the edge of the lower part of the upper, then use tack nails to attach the Seat to the bottom of the Last and apply some adhesive to the backside of the Seat that is showing and allow the adhesive to dry properly.

Hold the Last with one hand; press the back end of the Last firmly between your sternum and the top of your stomach. With the other hand, pull the upper over the body of the Last. The upper should cover over the Last with only the top of the Last sticking out.

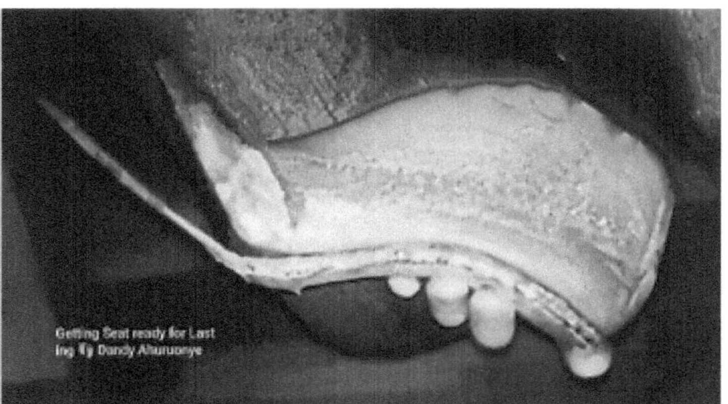

With the pincers, grip the tip of the lining just under the upper and pull forward until the upper fully resists the pull. This is the area that we said earlier that should not receive any adhesive. In one measured move, attach the lining material held between the pincers onto the Seat at the very top front of the Last.

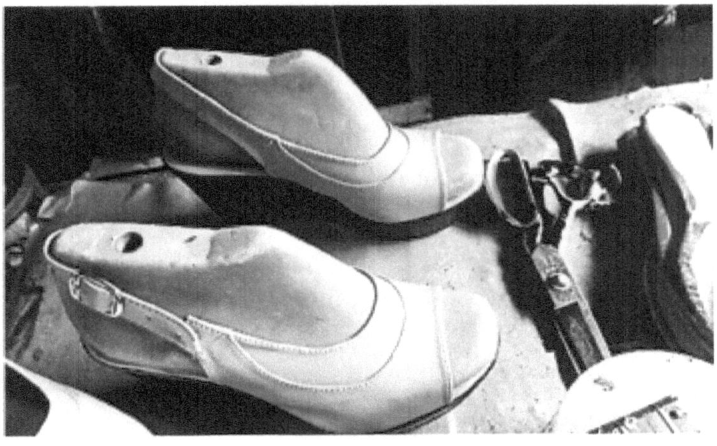

THE UPPER WILL NOW divide into two, with both the lining and the upper separated from the tip up to the edge of the third part.

At this point, we want to attach the upper onto the Last so they completely become one item. To achieve this, the tip of the upper must grip firmly on the front tip of the Seat. Then carefully use the pincers to attach both sides of the upper, just under the instep, to the Seat.

Attach the entire Top Line of the upper and lining with maximum force onto the Seat - including the rear part. Here, the Stiff will require much more force to get it to attach to the Seat.

We want the leather upper to be free - from the instep to the tip of the Last. Therefore, only the lining can be put on the Seat in this area.

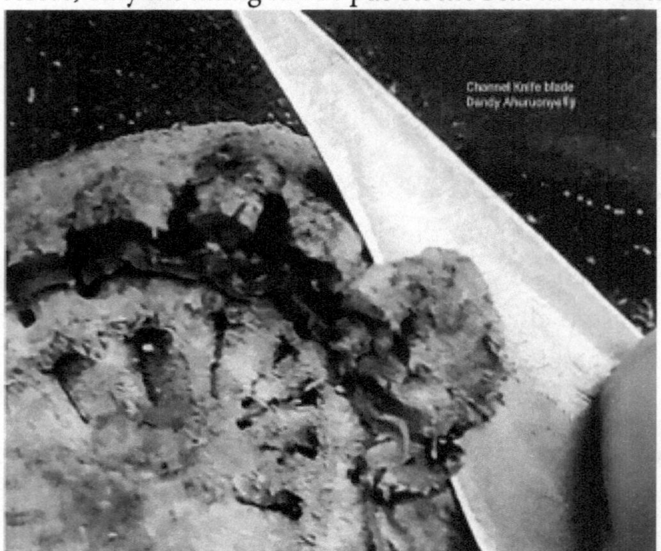

Use your sharp *channel* knife to cut off all the rough edges on the Seat or use the smoothing machine.

Apply some adhesive on the inside of the front Stiff, do the same on the front tip of the lining that is now resting firmly on the front of the Last, and allow both to dry fully.

The fore Stiff should not be longer than two to three inches; if the fore Stiff is too long, the edge of the Stiff will rub on the toes of the wearer and might cause friction and discomfort.

We know there can be issues with the shape and angle of some shoes because each person has a peculiar gait when walking. Just on this note, I know of certain shoe designers who, before building custom-made shoes for a wealthy client, watched her walk around for a while. He would afterwards take a hard look at her old shoes; he'll then combine his observations to determine her particular gait before setting out to build her a custom-made pair.

I tried this a few times successfully, but found it very tedious and extremely time-consuming. However, I also found that if one has the extra time, and the client is happy to pay the normally hefty price that is often attached to this extended special service, then that is a great opportunity for the designer to demonstrate his acute designing prowess and genius.

Well, I digress!

Now, returning to the application of the front Stiff, the next step is to hold the Stiff with both hands on two ends and place it on top of the front tip of the lining. Some Stiffs come in the shape of a triangle. Other front Stiffs are prefabricated and can be seen in various shapes. We will use this type with a triangular shape to make this pair. In that case, hold it on its two ends with the third pointing forward.

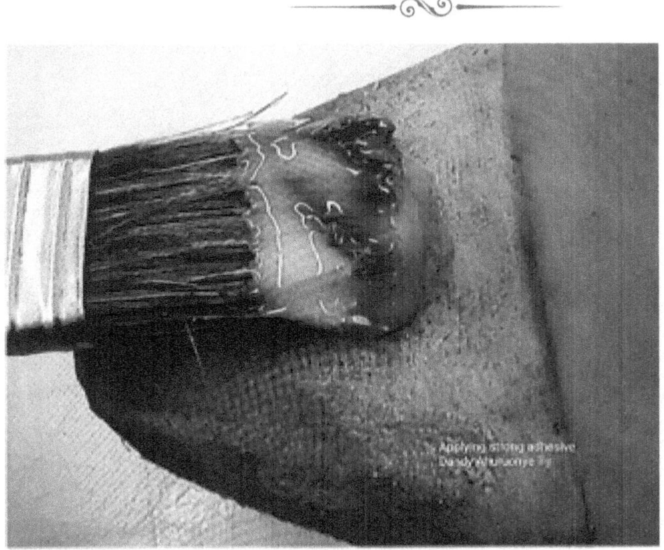

YOU MUST BE VERY METICULOUS here! Pay rapt attention and accurately determine where would be the correct position to place the Stiff; knowing full well that even the slightest mistake here would be impossible to correct, and may cause damage to the upper and requiring replacement.

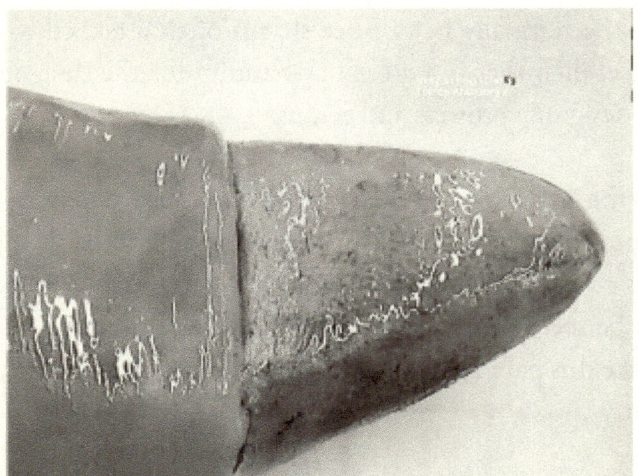

After you place the Stiff in the correct position and the right angle of the lining, use a mild heat treatment to gently soften the Stiff.

The Stiff must be soft enough to allow you to use your fingers or a plastic hammer to push it downwards until it becomes smooth and is fully resting on the lining.

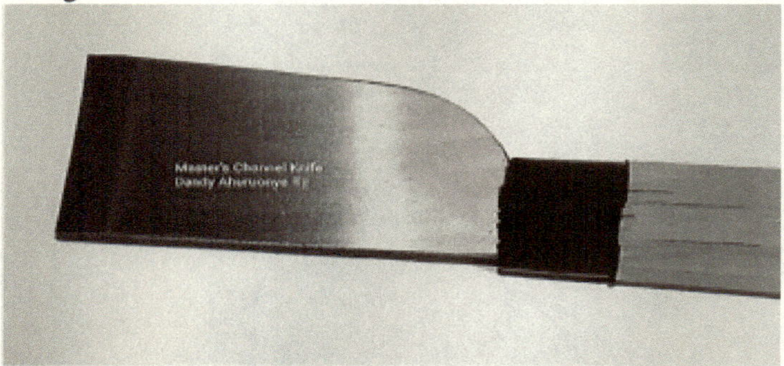

Use the knife to remove all excess material or bumpy spots; otherwise, use the smoother to make sure the Stiff is very smooth and has now become part of the lining. Apply some adhesive all over the lining/Stiff and the upper part that is sticking out and allow both to dry. Then with the pincers once more, hold the tip of the leather upper and repeat the same process as with the lining.

The goal here is to make sure that the entire upper is forced downwards to get it fully attached to the Seat and Last to become one item. The Lasting is now complete.

Before going any further, you must repeat the 'mirroring' process.

Leave the job alone for now and move away; do other things, go perhaps in a different room or outside the studio.

WHEN YOU HAVE RETURNED, take a hard critical look at the job you left on the table and see if you can identify any mistakes or imperfections. Look for bumps, rough edges, depressions, and dents, anything that might detract from your handwork.

Some hard-core designers may ask another designer or someone else to do the mirroring for them; because in the designing world, everyone knows that four or more eyes are always better than two. If you, your colleague, or your critic found anything that needs attention, then correct it before moving on to the next stage.

We will now install the other parts.

First, cut out a piece from the fibre material we used to prepare the Seat. This piece must be in the same shape as the front part of the Seat but one inch smaller in diameter all around.

In a slanted, outwards movement, use a smoothing machine or a sharpened knife to smooth all edges.

Place this piece on the front end of the Last to give a shape to the Seat and to boost the height by about half of a millimetre or less.

Next, apply glue all over the Nora sole and the Seat. Using extreme care and very steady hands, attach the sole to the Seat/Last – starting from the front of the Last.

It is worth noting that in some cases, the shoemaker may decide to use adhesive (gum) instead of glue to carry out this finishing process; however, there are no hard and fast rules regarding what kind of adhesive to use.

From my experience, high-quality glue is very durable and able to withstand lots of pressure from various elements like heat, cold, wet and oily conditions. Barge Cement is also reliable – if you can find some.

I must repeat the remark that there is no such thing as economising when handmade shoes are involved.

You must insist on the highest quality available for all parts of the footwear. The consensus in handmade products is that the superior quality of materials used will ultimately compensate for not using machinery.

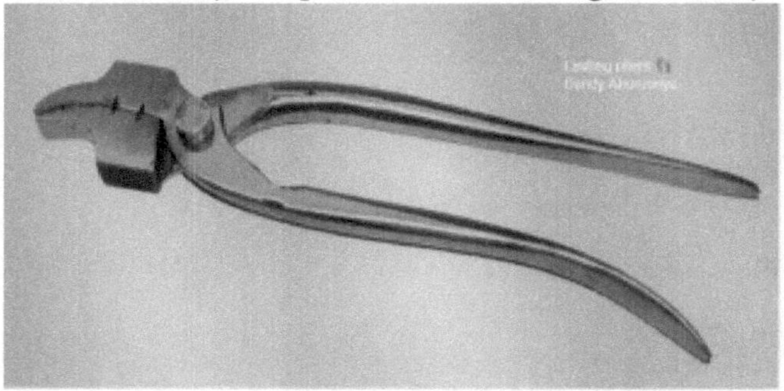

The adhesive is one of the most important components because it holds everything together, even when the other parts are of poor quality. If you cannot find a high-quality adhesive, use superglue to make the footwear. Glue, though, can be very difficult to use on all parts of the shoe simply because most types of glue products dry out soon after application.

To overcome this, it is necessary to look for certain types of glue that dry slowly. However, if everything else fails, then get the normal glue and apply it one bit at a time as you Last the shoes. This is highly recommended because - the assured quality of the final product will be worth the hassle and challenges of using glue to Last the shoes.

For our pair, we will carry out the Lasting using a very superior adhesive known as barge cement; this type can be imported from overseas.

Now that the Lasting is complete, we will attach the heel to the shoe.

First, apply the adhesive to both the heel and the rear of your footwear, and allow it to dry. Next, apply mild heat to both surfaces and then carefully install the heel. There is no harm in allowing some time after applying the heel before continuing.

Please remember that the shoe should remain on the Last during this process.

With the heel successfully attached, quickly put the shoe on a table and press down on the top of the Last just to make sure the heel sticks firmly to the shoe. You can also put a weighty item on the Last to speed up the setting process.

When I used to run my own designing studio, I would normally allow a few hours for them to set properly before trying to separate the Last from the shoe. Where the pair being built is a very expensive pair, leave the shoes attached to the Last for up to a day or longer, until the fine leather permanently assumes the actual shape of the Last.

After setting fully, you can now remove the shoe from the Last. This can be very tricky depending on the type of Last used, or how it was designed. If you used genuine professional-made plastic Last, then it is very easy to remove.

LOOK FOR A NARROW METAL pole, stick the metal pole into the hole at the top, near the rear of the Last and, in one swift move, hold firmly onto the pole and shift - forward-downward-outward and the Last is out of the shoe one or two seconds.

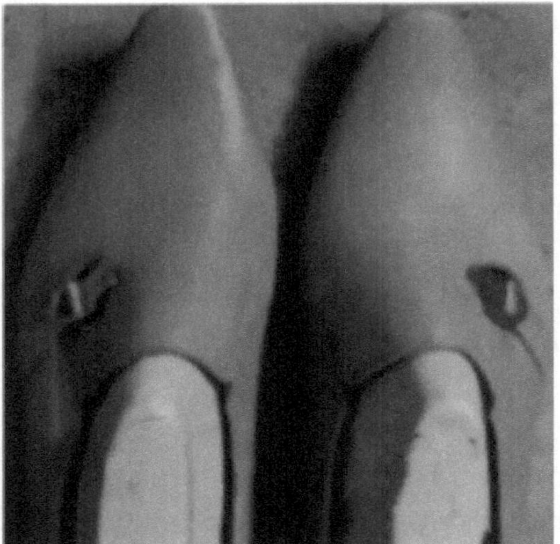

You must be sure that all required necessary steps are complete before attempting to manoeuvre the Last from the shoe. Once removed, it is very difficult to reattach the Last to the shoe. In addition, this can ruin the shoe or alter the shape negatively.

In the past, I experienced instances where the reattachment of a Last to the shoe caused irreparable damages.

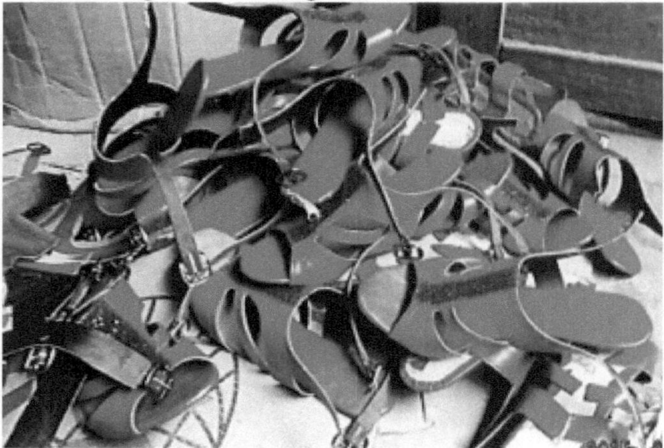

For those who are not fully trained in this manoeuvre, it is best if you applied a bit of talcum on the Last before carrying out the lasting process. The powder will help you detach the last with complete ease. With the shoe and Last now separated, it is time to secure the heels. Using a sharp metal awl, prick the rear of the Seat to locate the two holes drilled into the shank.

Then insert the screws and secure them firmly using a screwdriver. You must be careful here to avoid the screws going in the wrong direction and ruining the shoe by piercing the back of the heel.

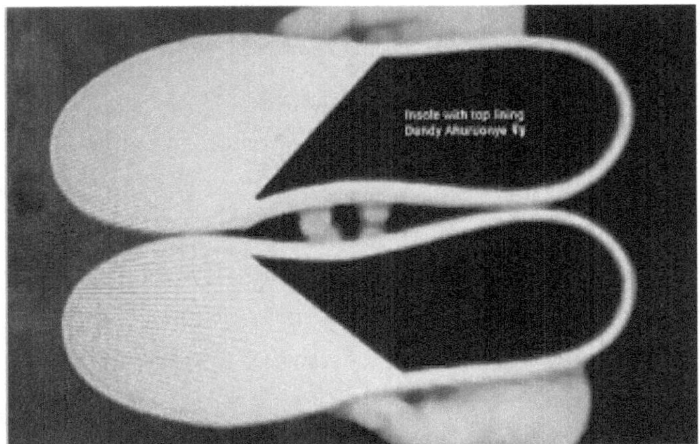

LABEL OR STOCK LINING

For the comfort of the end-user, it would be nice to apply a soft midsole on the Seat to give it a soothing mattress feel; a cork material is excellent for this purpose. Using the Seat pattern, mark and cut out material from a soft but superior insole lining and attach it to the Seat. The Stock Lining is the simplest part of the shoe to prepare, but must not be taken for granted.

Just use the Seat pattern to make a mark on the leather material, use a pencil for marking instead of a pen or marker to make sure the mark is very faint. You should use the same leather material that was used to prepare the inner lining of the upper. The reason for this is to give the inside of the shoe a matching presentation.

The last step is simply to insert the Stock Lining bearing the name or logo of the master designer onto the soft top seat or midsole.

After the mark, cut it out allowing about 2 cm outside the pencil mark. If you have a logo or insignia, now is the time to imprint or attach this hallmark to the Stock Lining.

Apply adhesive on the Stock Lining and the insole, allow to dry and apply mild heat.

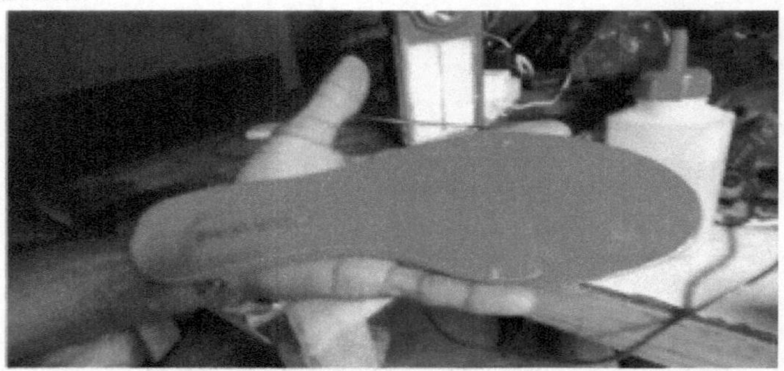

To attach the Stock Lining, first, place the shoe on the table, then hold the rear of the Stock Lining in one hand while holding the shoe in the other hand.

Attach the Stock Lining from the top of the Seat first making sure the Stock Lining covers the Seat well enough to hide it from view. Then slowly push the Stock Lining downwards toward the front of the shoe until fully bedded.

Check the shoe for stray adhesive and remove those with soft cloth made damp with kerosene or white spirit.

Our handmade pair of fine shoes is ready; congratulations to both the master designer and also our end user who is now in possession of a handmade bespoke pair of shoes. As we remarked earlier regarding products from one of the most celebrated shoe technicians of our era, this wearer will be *walking on air* from the very first minute she puts on a pair of Bespoke shoes!

DO NOT BE PUT OFF BY MISTAKES

From the day you set out to create and build your first pair of shoes, a single adversary will torment you; that enemy is the mistakes that you will inevitably make in every pair you will ever build. The best and most experienced shoe designers make mistakes every day, so take courage and do not despair if you find yourself making one mistake after another.

In the designing world, errors or perceived mistakes are acceptable. Some of the most popular footwear and other design concepts were born because the designer made a mistake in the studio while pursuing some other design.

Look at it this way - Assuming you had set out to build a pair of customised shoes that a client requested. She had described a design that you noted down on paper through a sketch. So you set out to conceive, prepare, and then design this pair. When she returned a few days later, she shocks you by saying that what you are making is so far detached from what she had in mind.

What are you going to do now? Well, of course, you will listen to your customer, note down whatever corrections she prescribes, and implement them. Ultimately, you want to please your client; you want to build exactly what she wants you to build. That is the hallmark of a skilled professional. There is also a principle involved here. If you fail this individual client, what makes you think you will please the next? But if you please her, well, the word will be out and another will come, and another, etc.

But what about the initial job that she rejected? Are you going to scrap or bin what you have already done? No! A good and resourceful craftsperson will improvise and convert this seeming mistake into a completely new design.

So, you could say that in this case, a mistake has led this shoemaker to produce a brand-new design that the world has never seen before.

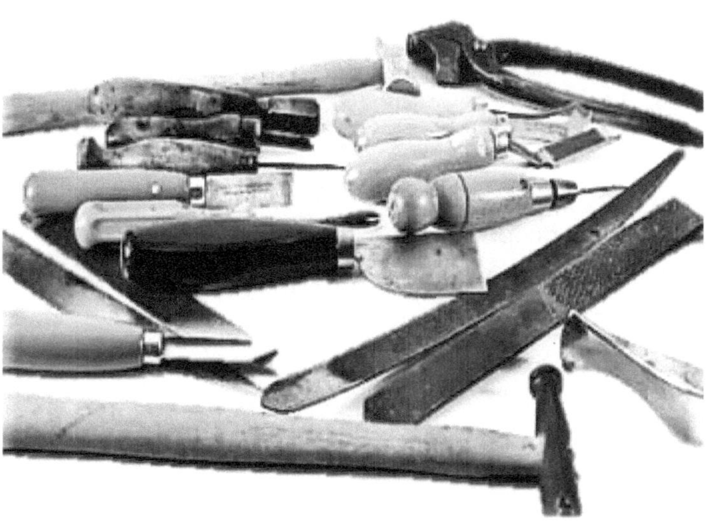

We could then say unequivocally that in designing there is no such thing as a mistake, simply because what those outside the industry would view as a mistake, is the birth of a new creation - a creation that no one has encountered before.

The parts mentioned already in this manual are not the only ones used to produce a pair of shoes. Depending on the design and finishing chosen, there are other important parts not mentioned, like – types of thread, laces, broaches, ornaments, studs, screws, ridges, Top Lines, stamps, Stock linings, glue, and buckles.

19: ABA CITY: AN INTRODUCTION

Aba, a medium-sized busy city in the East of Nigeria with millions of inhabitants, has, for many decades, been promoting the important craft of shoemaking by hand. Thus, I have elected to present its brief history. This introduction provides a glimpse of the challenges encountered by early shoemaking pioneers, and how they overcame these. The shoemaker, who has today colonised this city, had very modest beginnings.

A SHORT HISTORY

The city in the Southeast of Nigeria known as Aba, is the principal trading centre of Abia State. Aba started out as a small market town centre but was later established as a city by the Ṅgwà clan, who are the largest and most populous sub-ethnicity in this rural area of the southern Igbo plain; an area that makes up South- Eastern Nigeria. Not long after the British explorers arrived, the colonial administration established a military post there in the year 1901.

THE CITY IS AT THE intersection of a major route that leads to several other locations, including Ikot-Ekpene, Umuahia, Port Harcourt, and Owerri. The city became a collecting point for a good deal of rural produce, and products not long after Great Britain built a railway line that passed through the city to Port Harcourt. Within a short time, Aba developed into a major urban settlement. Some sections of the expanding city also became commercial centres. The main indigenous people or landowners of Aba are the Ṅgwà (Ngwa) tribe.

Aba city is well known because of the many craft workers who ingenuously produce many wares - from farming equipment to household items; and from clothes to footwear.

Aba, as a city, eventually became the administrative centre for the British colonial authorities.

Since then, Aba city has been a major commercial centre. Around the Last quarter of 1901, the British took up arms against the Aro forces, an Igbo group that was opposed to the British annexation of the Eastern peninsula of Nigeria and therefore resisted the perceived invaders. Around the years 1901 - 1902, some parts of the city felt the wrath of the colonial masters as they undertook extensive military action to quell all anti-colonial sentiments.

This military program, known as **The Aro Expedition**, was just one part of a wider military plan Britain had for the region. Even though the bold Aro forces held ground courageously for a while, in the end, they suffered terrible humiliation.

This outcome removed the myth of invincibility that had surrounded the Aro for a long time among the Igbo.

All this began after years of political and economic tension, crystallised by a fairly typical Aro hit-and-run attack on Obegu. Consequently, a formal military operation was launched against the Aro and their shrine of the Long Juju around the end of 1901.

A British Lieutenant Colonel H. F. Montanaro led thousands of officers, soldiers and carriers, from four stations, and advanced in an attack formation from locations including Itu, Oguta, and Akwete. What began as a sort of counter-insurgency campaign ended as a full-blown war that resulted in the blowing up of the reputed Long Juju shrine belonging to the Aro. Ultimately, this expedition, aimed at subduing the Aro, succeeded. Therefore, the slave trade routes managed by the Aro were stopped and destroyed.

After the military action proved a success, the British authorities quickly built a military outpost in Aba to help them maintain proper control of the surrounding areas and avoid a repeat of the Aro rebellion. From 1915, they began a major railroad construction project, intending to link Port Harcourt city with Aba. The decision to build a rail line would turn out to be crucial in helping Aba to develop as a city and a major commercial centre in this part of Nigeria. The rail service eventually helped the Ńgwà, and other surrounding peoples, to transport and exchange agricultural produce, and other local products.

As things turned out, though, the British realised that they still had much more work to do because, a few years later in 1929, a widespread revolt by Ńgwà and Igbo women engulfed Aba.

The Aba Women Riot was a symbolic response by the great cloud of female traders and artisans in the wider Aba area against the census of women in Aba; and some of the tax systems introduced by Britain. A protest that started as a peaceful demonstration soon mushroomed into a major riot. Nonetheless, by the 1930s, Aba was becoming a large urban community with an established industrial complex that catered to both male and female craft workers.

ECONOMY

Aba's proximity to Port Harcourt, thanks to the new rail network, helped the city in its development as a commercial centre. Several oil wells, some of which provided Aba with some kind of energy security at the time, surrounded both cities. Aba benefited from several economic contributors from such sectors as handicrafts, cosmetics, cement, palm oil, and textiles. Because of the several products and produce in and around Aba, many sections of the city developed into gigantic markets. These markets, in turn, attracted merchants and business people from all over the country and beyond.

One of these was the **Ekeoha Market**. This was an enormous market that kept growing in both fame and importance because of its impact on the entire economy of Aba as a city. The great Ekeoha fire of the 1970s eventually engulfed and destroyed this market. This fire incident had a profound negative impact on Aba, but also on the Igbo as a nation due to the collective importance of the market. Thousands of traders lost both their shops and their wares; this forced them to start all over.

The buyers also faced a terrible dilemma as they now had to travel to Onitsha or other distant locations to buy items they needed. So, it was no surprise that soon after this tragedy, city planners searched for a location to build a new market; and before long, they chose **Arịarịa (Ariaria) village** as the site of the new market.

In 1976, the first traders arrived in Arịarịa to erect their shops. Those pioneers were mostly timber dealers who then sold timber and other building materials to the next batch of prospective shop owners that had followed their lead. Most of these first arrivals had come from Ekeoha Market to make a fresh start in the wake of that great disaster they had encountered.

At first, no one gave Arịarịa any chance of success, mainly because they built the market around the site of a large swamp. Flooding and pools of water notoriously ravaged the area after each heavy rainfall. But even though many thought the new market would surely fail, the market soon became a pillar of economic success.

You could walk into Arịarịa market and buy anything from clothing to food, and from mechanical parts to building materials. The prices were also very competitive when compared to other markets. This helped Ariaria to become a major draw for merchants from all of West Africa. These buyers could purchase their needs either in bulk or in small quantities; so everyone headed to Ariaria for every need.

They divided Ariaria into special zones, with each zone providing a specific type of ware. They subdivided each zone into lines, and each line sold items grouped into that subsection. A-Line provided expensive, superior clothes and footwear, mostly imported from Europe, Japan, and North America. They also had other sections like the Medicine Line, Motor Parts Line, Home Ware Line, Foodstuffs Line, and so on. At its peak, the market had over one hundred zones.

The initial plan was for the new market to have around seven to ten thousand houses; each building was to accommodate three to five shops. Therefore, the plan was to have in the excess of forty thousand shops, which at the time sounded like a lot, as most people thought the new location would not even succeed.

Ariaria (Ariaria) Market, along with its surrounding areas, is currently estimated to have nearly two million traders, making it the largest single business district in the entire African region.

A market of this size can be very complex as a buyer must weave through a colossal maze of lanes, sub lanes, lines, sublines, sections, and subsections before locating where to buy what he is looking for. In recent years, street traders have added to the complexity of this market by selling their wares along the key roads, lines, and lanes that had originally been designed as major arteries to facilitate the flow of traffic.

The presence of the street traders (as seen in the above image), has choked the once wide market roads and lanes into narrow alleys.

This means that not only is it now difficult for the buyer to find what he wants to buy, but also traders individually waste several hours each day just to travel to their shops. However, this market is like other similar markets that operate elsewhere like those in China and India.

Ariaria imports tons of goods from around the world, while at the same time making and exporting all kinds of parallel items. Ariaria businesspeople imported such goods as machine parts, pharmaceuticals, shoes, men's and women's clothes, all kinds of homeware, and every kind of leather material from around the world.

Soon after opening its doors to the public, the market has been attracting customers from all over Nigeria, including such locations as Rivers State, Enugu, Akwa Ibom, Cross Rivers, and other states of Eastern Nigeria. But that was not all the interesting story about this vast market.

During the 1970s, a small cluster of shoemakers began to develop on the outskirts of the market along Faulks Road, which was the primary route that connected the city with Ariaria village. By the mid-1980s, it became a common sight to see traders and buyers from nearby West African countries like Niger, Gabon, Togo, Benin, and Cameroon. These would come in to buy some of the leather products, mostly footwear; and some buyers even came from as far away as Ghana.

During the late 1980s, the market experienced a large influx of these buyers from Cameroun. Traders from this neighbouring country became major buyers of leather products, particularly shoes manufactured in the market. The presence of the growing number of leather workers pivoted the market into a unique business centre.

WHAT BEGAN WITH A SMALL band of artisans in the early 1970s has now grown into a monstrous industry that churns out a million pairs of footwear every day.

Behind this massive success story was an insidious problem that - if not checked – was going to destroy this budding industry. But the problem was one that could only be tackled by either the local authorities or by the shoemakers themselves.

Faulks Road, Aba, August 1987

CHALLENGES FOR ARTISANS IN DEVELOPING LANDS

Artisans in many countries of the developing world are grappling with myriads of structural and infrastructural challenges. These include lack of, or infrequent electrical power supply, poor road networks, and an insatiable taste for foreign-made products that had become systemic.

Most shoemakers are at the entry-level of manufacturing; so, they do not have the necessary resources to provide their own machinery, including private power supply. They, therefore, depended on a power supply from the national grid to power the typically makeshift tools they use for their products.

When the power supply is down, which was a daily occurrence; It forced them to use tools that required no electricity. This limited what the artisan could accomplish.

Many retailers and personal users who normally bought locally made shoes, now preferred going to such places as China and Dubai to import shoes and other leather products. While this is understandably a welcome development for those countries, it was a piece of significant bad news for the local economy.

When locals fall into the trap of patronising foreign-made goods, it is only a matter of time before they realise that they have endangered the economic prospects of their own country. Buying foreign-made goods at the expense of locally made products can create a negative effect on the fight against high unemployment. The good news is that handmade shoes that are well made are usually of better quality than most of the imported ones. So, when locals buy locally made shoes, they are supporting local jobs, the local economy, and in doing so, they also have the assurance that the products they are buying are durable. Often, the buyer knows the shoemaker and so can return the product if the quality turned out to be suspect or poor. It might not be possible to do the same with products imported from overseas.

The underlying problem was that Nigeria was a country built on respect culture. To be esteemed, the rich and middle class sought to differ from everyone else by going to great lengths to dress up in foreign-made gear. It was taboo for any wealthy and financially comfortable person to buy the so-called **Aba-Made** products.

Therefore, the authorities could have looked for ways to alter the psyche of the citizenry, to persuade people to see that it would be in their best interest to buy items made in Aba. If they had done that, they would have supported homegrown industry and ingenuity, and that would have created jobs, lots of jobs.

However, this idea was just a utopia; no one cared anything about supporting the Arịarịa shoe industry.

Thus, it was up to the shoemakers themselves to come up with an idea to encourage their fellow Nigerians to buy Aba-made footwear. Aba-made shoes of the 1970s and early 1980s were good and had basic quality at affordable prices. This was fine for many poor people who could not afford imported shoes.

Nonetheless, with the increased arrival of higher quality shoes made overseas, it became obvious that the Arịarịa artisan needed to do more if he were to sell his products.

The clusters of the shoe artisan of the 1980s produced shoes that were slightly better than those of their 1970s predecessors. And equally, the shoemakers of the 1990s built footwear that had better quality than those from the 1980s who trained them.

Still, there was an obvious need to revolutionise shoemaking, not just in Aba, but all over Nigeria.

I was among the first shoemakers who realised the implications of the foreign-made footwear that were then becoming affordable. This realisation impelled me to rethink the business-as-usual model that was prevalent among local shoemakers in Aba, and indeed Nigeria.

A small group of artisans including me, met together to discuss this matter and afterwards decided to do something drastic to change the general perception that no one in Aba could produce durable shoes.

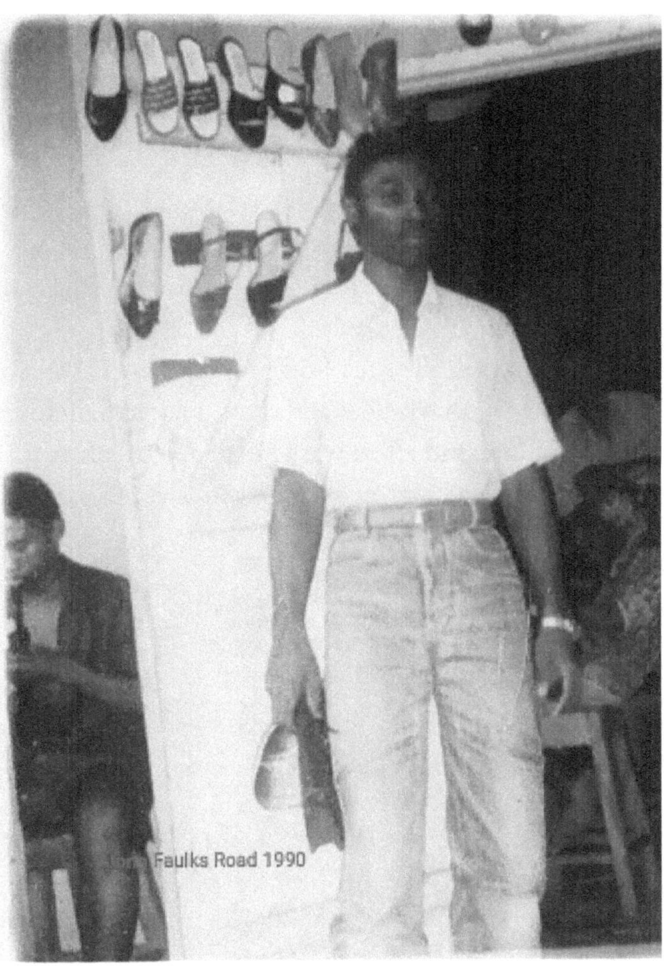

I HAD ORIGINALLY TRAINED to make sandals and other forms of basic footwear that were easy to build. But with the glaring challenge to wean the local consumers of their penchant for foreign goods, I decided that it was time to alter my approach.

This was a tough decision because of the known challenges of crossing from making one type of shoe to another. But once the decision was made, my focus now was on how to achieve this. It was always believed that producing the kind of footwear that would attract the middle class was reserved solely for the big-time footwear designers, and Aba probably had just two or three in those days.

I was willing to embrace the challenge, which was why, with no prior training or experience, I set out on my own to experiment with the designing and making of sophisticated covered shoes. It was a massive leap from producing sandals and slippers.

During that period, I used all the shoe manuals I could find, but I also received help from some of the few local designers who were already well established, like Sir White, Paucity, and Enon shoes. The first trial pairs of covered shoes I built turned out to be a disaster.

I found it very difficult to attach the back Stiff properly; my Lasting of the front tip of the shoe was riddled with wrinkles and spots. I left myself no choice but to promptly bin those. The second effort wasn't as bad as that first pair but wasn't particularly good either; yet I was determined to succeed, considering the effort I had already put in.

After everyone had gone home on some evenings, I would come back to my shop to continue all alone, tinkering away in the night's quiet.

SOON MY PERSEVERANCE paid off. Before long, I could build my first presentable pair of covered shoes. So, it turned out that I became one of the few people in those days who successfully migrated from making basic sandals to becoming a designer of covered shoes and boots.

Still, from my perspective, this was just the beginning as I aspired to become a top designer like the masters in Italy and Spain if I were ever going to change the reputation of Aba-made shoes. For a few times, I went to visit the industrial cluster strategy that had now been established in Ariaria when the United Nations Industrial Development Program (UNDP) opened a Common Facility Centre (CFC) for shoe manufacturers in Aba. This centre was the first of its kind in the Aba area. I was told at the time that the vision was to establish a CFC where the shoemakers in Ariaria would go to use specific machinery to finish their handmade shoes.

Business Card - circa. 1994

The argument was that by using machines to Last, couple, and finish their footwear, the final product would have a higher quality when compared to totally handmade shoes. They set the centre up to help the quality of Aba-made shoes to meet international standards. After a few visits, I decided that this centre wasn't for me, mostly because I was already making higher-quality footwear with my bare hands. I was convinced that I had mastered how to do it successfully without the need for those machines.

Dandy & Dandy Group Inc.
(WITH MBAHSON GROUP LTD)
General Designers/Merchants, Import/Export
Footwears, Dresses, Handbags, Portfolios
Briefcases, Sales/Services.

Dandy Aham Ahuruonye O Dip. (Hon) LDEP
President

Office/Showroom: *Overseas Contact*
7 Nwokejiobi Rd.   3958 Castro Vlly Blvd
Off 190 Faulks Rd.   Carlifonia 94546
Box.............Aba   U. S. A.
Abia State, Nigeria,

The CFC was a good idea; nonetheless, it also made the traditional artisan move away from the fundamental philosophy that was the foundation of the real Shoemaker. Industrial shoemaking is important as it provides the masses with affordable footwear. Without the large shoe industries, we might as well return to the ice age where people protected their feet with animal hides. Footwear would also be prohibitively expensive.

All that said, the art of shoemaking, is just exactly that - **An Art!** Yes, handmade footwear has its place in the world of creative art, alongside other greats as architecture, painting and sculpting. While the majority needed mass-produced shoes because of their availability and affordability, some others would not settle for anything else except handmade footwear. On the other hand, making shoes by hand is an industry of its own. This industry employs millions of people around the world - from India to Bangladesh; and from Nigeria to Egypt. Therefore, making shoes with bare hands is an industry that is here to stay.

There is that indescribable feeling that comes each time I finished building a pair of made-to-order shoes; each time I held up a shoe and admired its beauty. Nothing can describe this feeling; a person needs to experience it to be able to understand it.

I never experienced that same feeling after a few visits to the CFC, so I decided I would never again visit the Common Facility Centre. From that day I made up my mind to stick to using my hands as I have always done. I kept my promise and never went to the centre again.

Looking back, I am very pleased that I made that decision even though it was a hard decision, and seemed very foolish at the time.

WHY SHOEMAKING IS FOR EVERYONE

The consuming nature of the economy of many developing countries like Nigeria has harmed their effort to tame unemployment. Most consumer products used by the common people in these lands are imported from abroad.

They need to take a lesson from their rich counterparts considering that the manufacturing and industrial sectors are the key drivers for those economies. The US, Japan, The UK, Germany, and France all invested heavily in industry, especially Small and Medium Enterprises (SMEs).

Therefore, if Nigeria and other lands that make up the so-called third world countries are to reduce their high unemployment rate, shoe manufacturing factories and similar SMEs in Aba and other cities around the world must be recognised, and equally grouped in the same category as cement, oil, and steel industries.

If you are able to pay a visit to the shoemaking section of Arịarịa (Ariaria) Market, you can't help but marvel at the sheer size of this industry. There are people everywhere, people who are very busy 24 hours a day, seven days of the week. They conceive, design and produce all kinds of footwear. There you can see every design imaginable for both Gents, Ladies, and children.

Many of these shoemakers specialise in particular types of shoes; this is a welcome sight, especially when you consider that the unemployment rate in Nigeria and other developing lands is not in any way on the downward trend.

Often, the unemployment problem in these countries is exacerbated because of a progressive increase in the past few decades, in the number of graduates churned out annually by universities and other polytechnics of higher learning. Also, many students weren't able to further their education beyond the post-primary level; they too contribute to the swelling number of jobless youths.

If these countries are to achieve their aim of reducing the rate of poverty and joblessness, they must give urgent attention to the manufacturing sector, especially the SMEs where small-time shoemaking is grouped.

Governments can formulate essential policies that would discourage, or at least limit, the importation of foreign-made goods which can then be produced locally in their own country. They must train their citizens to proactively develop an affinity for locally made products. This will over time, not only create jobs for their graduates but will also boost their country's Gross Domestic Product (GDP).

The Chinese realised this very early on. At one point, they had to shut all the doors of importation in their homeland territory. Today, China is reaping the huge long-term benefit because of the sacrifices it had to make. It is very important therefore that those in the corridors of power should encourage the citizenry to start patronising locally made footwear.

There is a danger that the shoemaking industry might be looked down upon. Compared to other industrial sectors, shoemaking is a tiny industry. However, small economies can invest in and develop SMEs to encourage the educated jobless to consider the option of entering this sector. Some graduates might be discouraged because of the possibility of having to retrain, but they should also realise the huge potential in leather work. The reality where millions of graduates and other school leavers hang around or loiter all over the place with nothing to do is very dangerous.

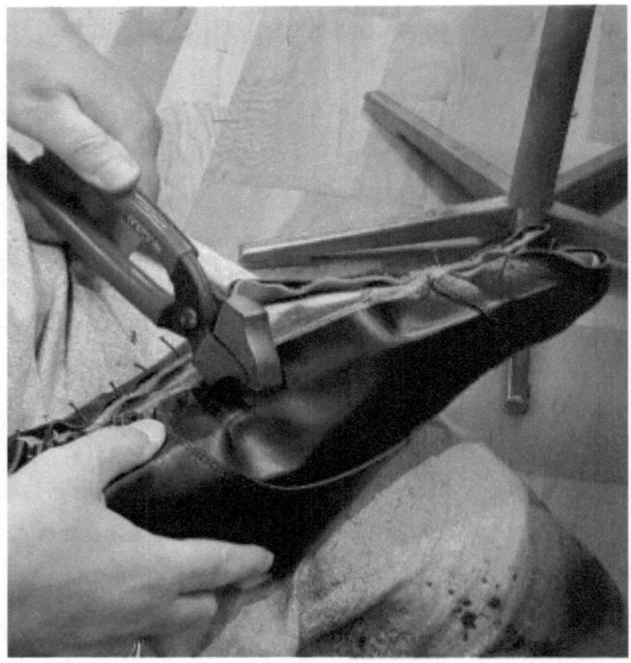

Many of these believe that jobs will come on stream soon. Others feel that there is some kind of stigma attached to becoming a shoemaker. The fact is, though, that these youngsters go from one year to another sitting around, and hoping for a job that most likely won't come. On the other hand, training to become an artisan adds a crucial dimension to the flexibility of the college graduate.

Many graduates leave the university with a wealth of head knowledge but no hands-on experience to back it up. Shoemaking provides a quick solution to that lack of practical experience.

Shoe designing is an important industry, but also a very easy craft to master. I have known some clever individuals who trained from having no experience whatsoever to becoming full-fledged designers in just nine months. So those with a university education will find it very easy to train as artisans since they would normally have a strong background in intensive study. In fact, with a book like this one, the graduate could choose to teach himself or herself how to become a Shoemaking guru.

All that would be required then is for this person to receive financial and infrastructural backing, and he's ready to banish his unemployment woes.

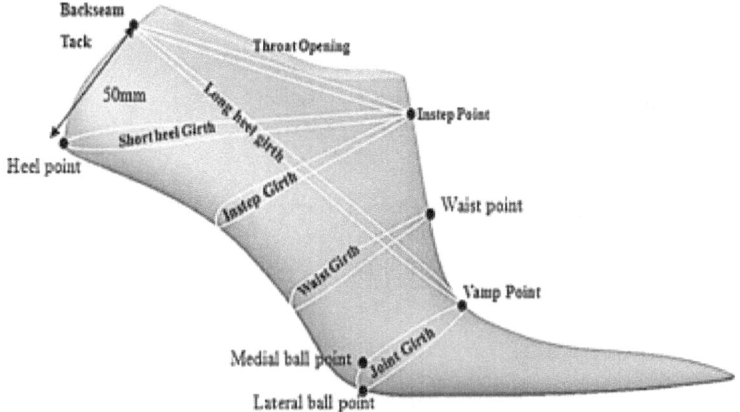
Backseam
Tack
Throat Opening
50mm
Long heel girth
Short heel Girth
Instep Point
Heel point
Instep Girth
Waist point
Waist Girth
Vamp Point
Medial ball point
Joint Girth
Lateral ball point

20: WHY WE NEED A SHOE MANUAL

There are many reasons why handmade shoes are very difficult to make and, by implications, very expensive to purchase. The reason, as we outlined at the outset, is that the designer has to be trained extensively before he or she can become a Tailor, Machinist, Smoother, Knitter, Laster, and Coupler all at once to competently design and build a pair of shoes without the use of mechanical equipment. Consequently, handmade shoes require special skills if they are to have good quality and look presentable. In this book, I have tried to show you how to produce a pair of fine shoes by hand with minimal - if any - use of machinery.

I want you to become the designer; to become highly trained and able to either carry out all the actions required to produce a pair of shoes, or be in a position where you can direct someone else on what to do to achieve the same result. Each person seriously contemplating becoming an independent shoe designer should have a copy of this guidebook.

This manual helps professionals to realise that it is possible to produce footwear of various designs without relying too much on an electric power supply or some expensive machinery. As already highlighted, one of the main uphill tasks that shoemakers in the developing world face, include the deplorable state of the electrical power supply.

I urge both unemployed individuals and the policymakers in the corridors of power to consider investing in this sector. Shoemaking is a craft that would hardly let anyone down, as people are always going to wear shoes. And as noted already, footwear comes in various moulds, which means that a certain type caters for a certain need. The only concern is whether the quality of their product would be good enough for people to rely on them.

This then is where those in power can make a crucial intervention by providing incentives like student loans, power supply, and a localised drive to encourage locals to patronise locally made products. In such a scenario, everybody wins. So, let's take the first plunge - use this manual to start the first of the three crucial watchwords of becoming a shoemaking professional - Practice! Once you practise, then take the subsequent steps - practice and practice some more. This would certainly help you become the shoe designer that you didn't realise you were. Your aim must be to train yourself on how to build fine and durable footwear.

Yes, by following these time-tested principles and guidance from an experienced professional, you too can successfully create fine footwear........

.... *One Pair at a Time!*

21: MORE ACKNOWLEDGEMENTS

THANK YOU:

Rachel Ahuruonye for being a noble wife; for her love and encouragement.

My beloved daughters, Joy Chinwendụ Ahuruonye, and Ruth Chidiebere Ahuruonye, for their inspiration.

My beloved brother, Justice Ụzọndụ Ahuruonye, who has proven to be my tireless supporter through the days of distress – Uzor, you are worth many brothers!

Thank you Mr Hillary Amaram for all your firm counsel.

Mr David Amalaha and Udochi Enweremmadụ.

Cherechi Suzanna Akaole

Amarachi Ahuruonye

Chidindụ Godspower

Pa Marcus Ahuruonye

Okezie Shadrach Ahuruonye and everyone in his family – including Anụrị & Peter Ugoọji, Chidi, and Ogechi.

ALL members of the Ahuruonye Ikpefu, and Nwokocha families.

Special recognition to my uncle, Prof. Benson Omenihu Oluikpe

I would also like to mention:

Abigail and Mezie (Meeme); Daa Rose, Nkechi, Chinyere, and Ebere – We will always remember all of you.

Also worthy of remembrance are:

My Late friend, Peter Nkọrọ (Aba)

The Late Rufus Nwakamma (Aba)

The Late Steven Ejinwa (Aba)

Thanks to my late grandparents:
Elizabeth Nwachukwu
Pa Moses Nwachukwu.

THANKS TO MY LOYAL FRIENDS, STAFF, & MENTORS:

Mr Victor Ọpara, Nelson Nwokejiobi, Christopher Nwachukwu

Chinenye Adiele, Christian Chigbundu, Charlie Anọruo

Eunice Ụgbọ, Onyebuchi Eze, Emeka Chianụ, Joseph C Akwarandụ

Uzọma Ụwaọma, Chuby Amaechi

Godwin Nwachukwu, Monday Bekee (Sir Momo)

Confidence Ogụeri, Sunday Onwụbụ

Esther Ọnụọha

Prof Temple Nwokocha

Mr Aaron Brown (Fettercairn, Tallaght)

Chief Amadi Akaraka Ahuruonye

John Ọhaneje, Grace Okorie, Onyebuchi Eze

Emmanuel Ngọzi Nwokocha,

Ezekiel Egbu

Agnes Neveu – Brittany, France

Harmony Onyehide, Capt. John Douglas Hume

Sir White & Paucity

Special thanks to:

Mr Fyne N. Emmanuel, Abuja

Mr Micah Mgbeahụrụ for all the guidance and counsel

AUTHOR PROFILE:

Dandy Ahuruonye has published material that delves into such wider spheres as current affairs and social issue commentaries. In recent years, he has written articles, lectures, technical materials, short stories, books, and critiques. Many of these are published on various platforms and are accessible to the general public.

Ahuruonye was born in Aba, Nigeria, and has spent much of his adult life in Europe. His father was Friday Enwereji Ahuruonye; one of the many children of a tribal ruler – Chief Ahuruonye Ikpefu. His mother was Madam Joy Chinagorom Ahuruonye.

He started his education at Umuikaa Central primary School soon after the Biafran war and later moved to Mkpuka Community Primary School. After his primary school education attended St Ephraim Secondary School Owerrinta. Ahuruonye subsequently completed his studies at the Dublin Institute of Technology, Ireland. He holds a diploma in Fashion Designing and a University Certificate in Medical Records from DIT (HMI).

Dandy has published several books including a technical work on fashion and designing: "The Shoemaker - Principles and Guide for Professionals." He has also published a host of children's books including: 'Illustrated Children's Stories;' 'Groccoli;' 'Waka;' 'The Good and Ugly Weather Friends;' 'The Eel and Phil in Kill;' 'The Grass Fart in Donegal Bay.' His most prominent work is the 600-page encyclopaedia: The Whispering Poet – An Anthology of Igbo & Other Proverbs.

THE SHOEMAKER:

Principles & Guide
For Professionals

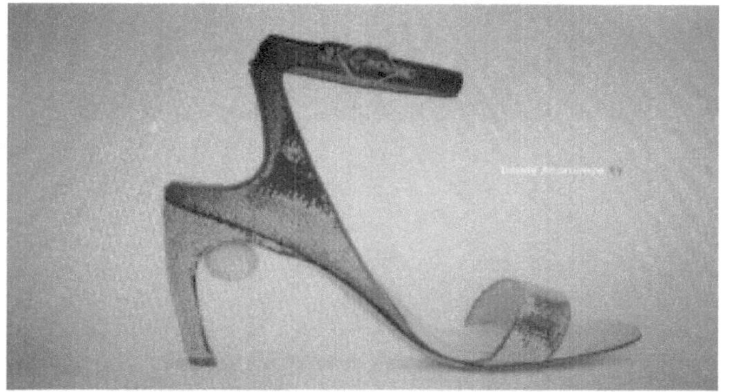

Dandy Ahuruonye Books
A PEN'S MIGHTIER THAN THE SWORD

Also by Dandy Ahuruonye

THE WHISPERING POET: An Anthology of Igbo And Other Proverbs
Grocc-ofly
Reading Glasses for Mama Eagle
The Cute Kids of Madugascar
Nora never gave up
A Fishhook and the Riverboy
Positive Brainwash
Groccolli
The Adventures of Groccolli
Happyville
Oh, What a Mars!
Stinky and The Dung Beetle
The Gull Who Must be Obeyed
THE SHOEMAKER: Principles & Guide for Professionals

Watch for more at https://wordpress.com/home/
dandyahuruonye.wordpress.com.